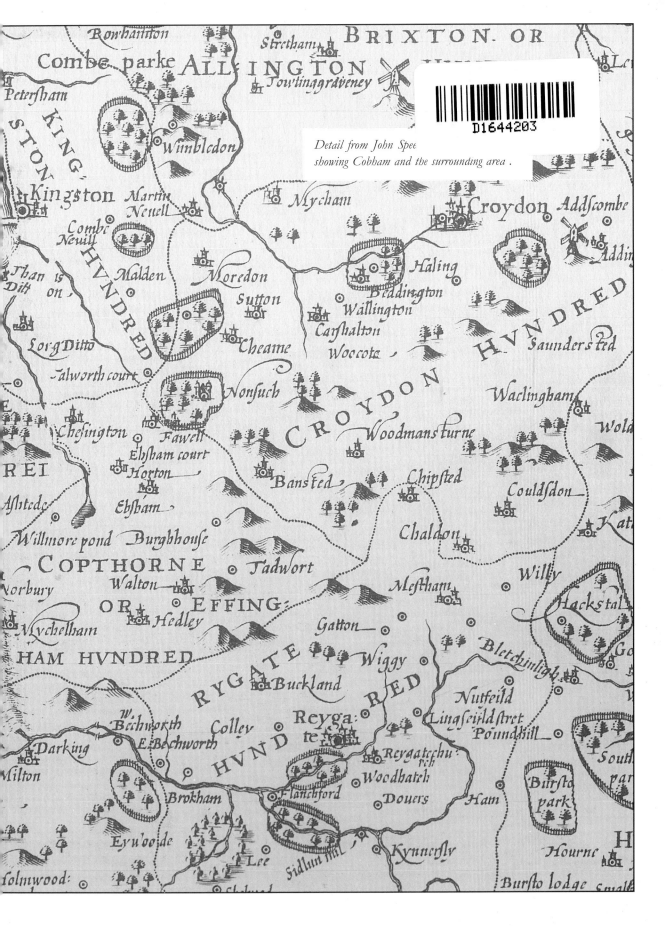

Detail from John Spee[...]
showing Cobham and the surrounding area .

COBHAM

A HISTORY

This early 20th-century postcard of Cobham High Street shows the view towards River Hill. Gammon's store (now the site of Cobham Furniture) is on the left and Kippins shop and the Fox and Hounds *pub are on the right. Nearly all these buildings were demolished for road widening in the 1960s. The only building still standing is that on the right, facing the end of the High Street, which is now La Capanna.*

COBHAM

A HISTORY

David Taylor

Phillimore

2003

Published by
PHILLIMORE & CO. LTD
Shopwyke Manor Barn, Chichester, West Sussex, England

ISBN 1 86077 247 1

Printed and bound in Great Britain by
THE CROMWELL PRESS
Trowbridge, Wiltshire

CONTENTS

LIST OF ILLUSTRATIONS

Frontispiece: Early 20th-century view towards River Hill

INTRODUCTION

Cobham is not one of England's historic showpieces, nor does it contain much to distinguish it from any other similar sized community. However, it does have a long and varied history making it different from any other place and thereby providing a strong sense of identity of its own. I suppose that by virtue of its size, density and population it must now be regarded as a small town. However, to many, myself included, Cobham remains 'the village'. It is the place in which I have lived all my life and to which my mother's parents came during the early years of the First World War. It is a place with a lively community at its heart made up of many people whose families have, like my own, been here for two, three or more generations.

Through the wholesale destruction of much of the individual character of our towns and cities over the past fifty years, we have become painfully aware of our need for buildings, landscapes and communities with which we can identify and where we feel at home. This has been underlined by the meteoric increase in interest in both genealogical research and local history. Civic and conservation societies are stronger today than ever before, as we become aware of our surroundings and the need to preserve the best of the past and replace the old and worn out using the best of modern-day skills and craftsmanship.

In 1982 I was invited to write the first ever published history of Cobham. *The Book of Cobham* is now out of print. During the course of the last 21 years there have been many new discoveries concerning both the origins of Cobham and its later development. This includes not only the physical legacy of old buildings but also the richly varied and colourful lives of many of the people who have lived here and made it their home. *Cobham – A History* is a complete revision and of that first book, taking into account many of those discoveries and revised theories, especially those concerning the early history of Cobham. It will sit comfortably alongside *Cobham Houses and their Occupants* and the other books which I have written dealing with various aspects of our local history. I hope that through the book you will see something of the continuity of history in Cobham, of the acting-out of national events on the local scene. It is also my hope that it will lead to a deeper appreciation of the community not only for what it has been in the past, but also for what it can be in the future.

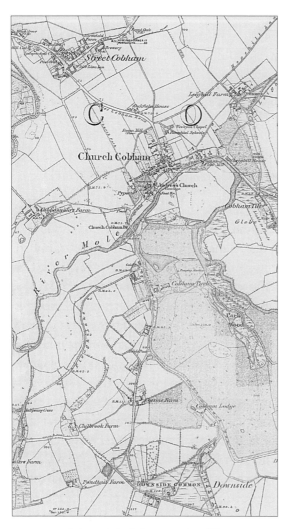

I   *1st edition 6-inch O.S. map, 1870. The separate settlements of Church Cobham and Street Cobham can clearly be seen, kept apart by the Church Field and linked by Street Cobham Road (now called Between Streets).*

The 20th century is still very much the recent past and a few more years need to pass before a fully objective account of that period can be written. With this in mind I have deliberately kept the closing chapter to a synopsis of the events of the past one hundred years.

I am very grateful to so many people who have assisted me in my researches over the years and to the many friends who have both inspired and encouraged me as I have researched our history. In particular I wish to acknowledge firstly the truly important pioneering work of my teacher, mentor and friend, the late T.E. Conway Walker FSA, and secondly my wife Carrie, without whose patience, understanding and support the book could not have been written. I am also deeply grateful to the expert advice that I have received from Dr Andrew Bradstock, Dr David Bird, John Pile, Dennis Turner and Dr David Robinson, all experts in their own fields. I should also like to acknowledge the ongoing courteous help and and patience of Mrs Margaret Vaughan-Lewis, the County Archivist, and all her staff at the Surrey History Centre. I believe that what I have written is both true and accurate but any errors or omissions of fact or attribution that may have occurred are entirely my own responsibility.

One

EARLY DAYS

'A Creature of the Mole'

The name of a city, town or village will often provide a clue as to both its early history and the reason for its geographical position. Cobham was once described as 'a creature of the Mole' and the settlement does seem to owe its present name to its position in a large distinctive bend of the River Mole. Until as late as the 18th century it was still often referred to by its old name of Coveham or Covenham. There are several possible origins for the name Covenham. Ham(m) is either the Old English *hām*, meaning homestead, or *hamm*, meaning land hemmed in by water. Cove could also refer to the bend in the river between the crossings at Downside and Street Cobham. This was well-watered land worth cultivating. Another possibility is that the original name was either Cofa's ham(m), where Cofa is a personal name, or cofa ham(m), where cofa means 'inner chamber', which could refer to Cobham Court, the manor house which sits centrally within the loop of the river. The old name for the River Mole was 'Emele' or 'Emlyn'. The name 'Mole' only appears in the 16th century and is referred to as such in Spencer's *Fairie Queene*.

Cobham is now regarded as a single entity comprising Street Cobham and Church Cobham, which were once separate communities. Street Cobham developed around the old Portsmouth Road, where it crossed the River Mole, and Church Cobham grew up around the parish church of St Andrew. These two communities were kept apart by the old common fields but linked by the aptly named Between Streets. It is unlikely that that part of the parish called the Tilt was, as a local schoolmaster once suggested, a place where medieval knights held their jousting tournaments. The name comes from the Saxon word *tilthe* which suggests this was land under the plough at an early date. To the south of Cobham is the hamlet of Downside which takes its name from the hill, or down, which rises steeply from the river within the present Cobham Park. Downside is now a part of the neighbouring parish of Ockham.

Geography

The original parish of Cobham was one of the largest in Surrey, covering some 5,300 acres and with a current population of a little over 10,000. The ancient parish originally included parts of Oxshott and Downside and was bounded by the ten ancient parishes of Walton, Esher, Thames Ditton, Kingston, Stoke D'Abernon, Little Bookham, Effingham, East Horsley, Ockham and

2 *The severe floods of 1968 caused the collapse of the middle section of the old Downside Bridge.*

Wisley. Surrounded by commons to the north-east and farmland to the south and west, Cobham has managed to retain its own identity although Downside is now clipped by the M25 motorway and further threatened by a service station and new rail link. The core of the old village around the parish church and by the River Mole has survived and is now one of four conservation areas to be found in Cobham.

Geology

Cobham is an area of low geographical relief. In the north-west, the River Mole flows at a level less than 50 feet above sea level and only a small area of Oxshott Heath reaches a height of 225 feet. The soils of the parish are chalk, London Clay, gravel and the alluvial soils and Bagshot Sands that can be found on Oxshott Heath. Fossil sea creatures found in the London Clay are a reminder that once this area was under water. There is no shortage of surface water passing through the parish from the River Mole's large catchment area in Surrey and Sussex, and this accounts for the sometimes heavy seasonal flooding. The flood plain is at its widest south of the river and this was clearly seen in the

severe and destructive flooding that occurred in 1968, when Downside Bridge was washed away and most of the open land on that side of the village took on the appearance of an enormous lake.

While the course of the Mole has been a crucial factor in the siting of Cobham, the two river terraces, or levels, which are particularly evident in the area, have been just as important in the siting of individual buildings. The edge of the Lower Terrace is prominent around Cobham Tilt and by the mill. The wisdom of our ancestors is clearly demonstrated in the siting of some of Cobham's oldest properties, such as Cedar House, The Old Mill House, Millwater Cottage, Ham Manor and the parish church which, despite their close proximity to the river, have remained largely unaffected even during the severe flooding of 1968.

The more ancient habitable sites of Cobham Park, Painshill and the Fairmile mark the Higher Terrace, which is the older. High proportions of sand and gravel are found in the upper terraces. The gravel deposits on the Fairmile Common were once much in demand for road making and large pits were opened up close to the Portsmouth Road.

Although most have long since been abandoned, the disturbed hummocky ground can still be seen. In 1822 Joseph Denby applied to the parish for leave to have part of the gravel pit at Fairmile to build a cottage, 'he being a pauper belonging to this parish.' Leave was granted and Denby Road, near the Tartar Hill, now marks the site. Another gravel pit existed on the slopes of Leigh Hill and, in more recent years, gravel was extracted from this area for the construction of the Esher and Cobham by-pass.

Cobham is an area of low rainfall, the annual average being 25 inches. The prevailing moisture-laden winds from the south-west deposit heavy rain first on the South Downs, then on the Leith Hill range, and finally on the North Downs before reaching Cobham. It has been suggested that rainfall was much greater in Roman times, and areas such as the Tilt, which are even now liable to flooding, were probably once marshland.

The Stone Age and the Bronze Age
Remains of nomadic prehistoric man have been found in different parts of Cobham and in 1965 a flint axe from the Mesolithic period (8500-3500 BC) was discovered near the river. Other flint scrapers and implements have been found in the grounds of Pyports, an old house that stands opposite the parish church. A polished flint axe from the Neolithic, or late Stone-Age, period (4000-2000 BC) was found near Norwood Farm in 1968 and, more recently, another small flint axe from this period was found on the Leg O'Mutton Field in the centre of Cobham. This may have been used for fine work or was possibly purely for votive or ceremonial purposes. It was in the late Stone Age that plant cultivation and

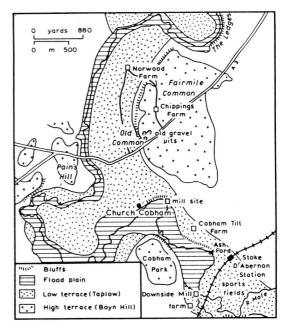

3   *The terraces of the Mole around Cobham.*

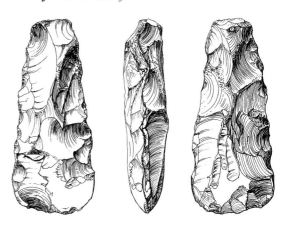

4   *Mesolithic flint axe found on the Leg O'Mutton Field.*

animal husbandry were introduced into southern England, and woodland was opened up to create fields for growing crops.

A burial from the period known as the Bronze Age (2000-700 BC) was discovered in a small gravel pit in the grounds of Leigh Court on Leigh Hill at the beginning of the last century. The burial consisted of a cremation urn about five inches high. Sadly,

5   *Bronze-Age urn found at Leigh Hill.*

the workmen who discovered it, in the vain hope of finding treasure, emptied out any human ashes the urn may have contained. Fragments of a 'hanging bowl' were found close by in the garden of Leigh Hill House. Further limited excavations of the sites have taken place in more recent times.

An Iron-Age site at Leigh Hill

During the Iron Age (700 BC-AD 43) period a large number of hill forts were constructed throughout England and Wales. The nearest of these to Cobham is at St George's Hill, Weybridge. Although their function is not entirely understood, it is likely that the close proximity of the fort on St George's Hill would have had a significant effect on the lives of the surrounding scattered farming communities such as Cobham.

The first known settlement in Cobham appears to date from about this time and was evidenced by discoveries made on Leigh Hill in the early years of the last century when a driveway was being constructed to the now demolished 'Appletons', a large Edwardian house that once stood here. The site revealed a number of circular gravel pits whose purpose was at first uncertain. It was thought the pits had been used as fireplaces and refuse pits but, as excavation proceeded in 1907, evidence of hut circles was found which, when compared with similar sites in other parts of the country, seemed to date from the Bronze or early Iron Age. The Leigh Hill site produced fragments of hand-made and wheel-made pottery, the latter dating from the Roman period. There were also loom weights and primitive weaving apparatus and pot-boilers, such as would have belonged to a British settlement of this type. The primitive houses of the people who lived here would have consisted of circular walls covered by low, thatched roofs supported by wooden posts and with a central hearth.

6   *The Iron-Age settlement at Leigh Hill probably looked similar to this reconstruction of an excavated settlement at Tongham. (From* Hidden Depths *by Roger Hunt and others.)*

Two

THE ROMANS

It was once believed that, when Julius Caesar and his army made their second expedition to these islands in 54 BC, they crossed the Thames at Coway Stakes in nearby Walton on Thames and passed close to Cobham. However, this theory is no longer accepted. When the legions came again in AD 43 under General Aulus Plautius, they probably landed on the south coast near Chichester and marched up through present-day Sussex and Surrey passing close to Cobham.

The Roman Occupation of Surrey

At this time most of the area that forms modern Surrey fell within the tribal area of the Atrebates. These people seem to have put up little resistance to the Romans and may well have actually welcomed the invaders. The major Roman legacy in southern England is a superb network of long straight roads converging on their new city of Londinium. Although those living south of the Thames seem readily to have accepted the Romans, the tribe of the Iceni in East Anglia led by Queen Boudicca challenged their exploitation of her area. In AD 60 Boudicca and her warriors sacked London and it seems quite likely that after the destruction of the capital her jubilant army would have continued heading south and

perhaps passed through our area before meeting its end on the road to Silchester, perhaps near Virginia Water.

In addition to the Romano-British settlement that continued the occupancy of Leigh Hill, there are at least two other significant Roman sites in Cobham. During the construction of sewage works near Cobham Bridge in 1932, Roman pottery and wattle and daub fragments were found which indicated a settlement with timber huts in *c.*AD 50-100. Sainsbury's superstore now covers this site. It is possible this was the site of a farmstead that may have been contemporary with the other site at Chatley Farm.

Roman Bathhouse at Chatley Farm

Chatley Farm is at the southern end of the parish and lies on the east of Ockham Common, between the sands of the common and the rich alluvial soil by the River Mole. The remains comprised a bathhouse of the Roman period of *c.*AD 350. Bathhouses are usually found in connection with a nearby villa or industrial process, such as the tile manufactory at nearby Ashtead. However, no such building has yet been discovered on the Chatley Farm site and it may well be that the river has destroyed any villa that may have existed together with about a third of the bath building. Bathhouses were sometimes free-standing but have also been found added to pre-existing buildings.

The Chatley Farm building was first noticed in June 1942 and subsequently excavated by the Surrey Archaeological Society. It proved to be a normal bathhouse of which four rooms had survived. These were a cold bath of roughly semi-circular shape, a *tepidarium*, or warm room, a *calidarium*, or hot room, and a sweating chamber constructed over the usual under-floor heating system provided by a hypocaust chamber. This last room was subsequently altered to house the boiler. It is possible that at least one other room once existed at the northern end which acted as an entrance hall and undressing room. The archaeologist Professor Sheppard Frere considered that the

building was of poor construction and that it ceased to be used soon after AD 360. He concluded, 'Its end may have been brought about by the raids of the Picts, Saxons and Irish which were a notable feature of that decade.' In other words, the building may have been sacked or the owners fled, leaving it to fall into decay.

Finds from the excavation at Chatley Farm included a variety of pottery and pattern-stamped flue tiles together with 16 coins that suggested the building was in use *c*.AD 320-60. Fifty years after the bathhouse was last used, the legions left Britain to return to Rome and the remaining population was left to face the increasing invasions from across the North Sea.

In September 2003 members of the Surrey Archaeological Society undertook a field walking survey of the area around the Chatley Roman site. This found no evidence of any

7 *Chatley Farm, Downside.*

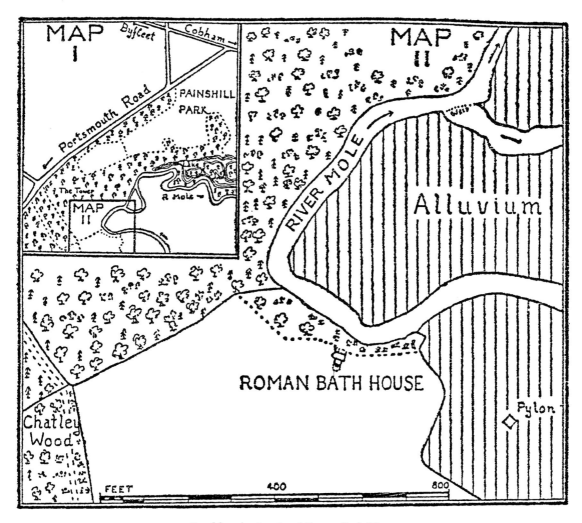

8 *Map showing site of Roman Bath House.*

other buildings, which seems to confirm that the villa associated with the bath house is likely to have been washed away by the action of the river. A coin of Magnentius (AD 350-353) found at this time points to the bath house dating from the fourth century.

Other Roman sites

The Chatley Farm building and the evidence of occupation on the Sainsbury's site may point to the existence of a Roman road in this area. Just as the Romans constructed other roads leading towards London such as Stane Street, it is possible that a road running from Winchester, which has been traced as far as Farnham, might have passed through Cobham, fording the River Mole here. Such a road could have followed a natural valley running through Painshill Park instead of following the present route up the steep incline out of Cobham towards Guildford. The Chatley site is also close to a suggested Roman road from Farley Heath

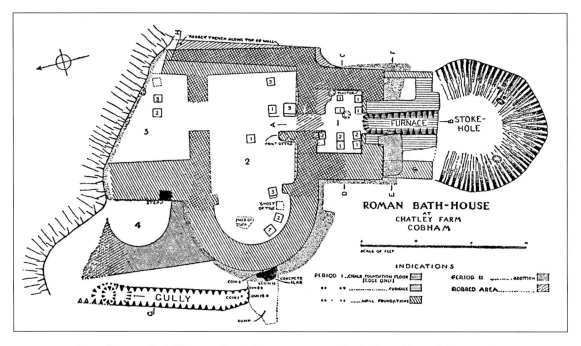

9 *Plan of Roman Bath House at Chatley Farm as excavated by Professor Sheppard Frere in the 1940s.*

to St George's Hill and the Thames at Walton. This road may have been the Eldelane (Old Lane) or Stonilane that is referred to in the perambulation of the bounds of Cobham found in the Chertsey Cartulary. Old Lane is still the name for a road running through Hatchford by the *Black Swan*.

According to the Cobham *Parish Magazine* of April 1934, a boy bathing at Pointers found a Roman silver coin. In 1932-4 Mr Edward Partridge of Chilbrook Farm found four Roman coins in Plough Meadows. One of these was from the time of Constantine I whilst two others were from the time of Constantinus II. A bronze coin of Constantine II was found in the garden of a house in Tilt Road in 1958. Roman tiles found in the fabric of Stoke D'Abernon church have led to speculation that a Roman building lies under the Manor House lawn, but this has yet to be proved and the tiles may well have come from the Chatley Farm building. A small building with possible religious significance was excavated near *Woodlands Park Hotel* some years ago.

Three

SAXONS AND NORMANS

In the fifth century AD Saxons settled the south east of England in a process that is still not fully understood. The traditional picture of conquest by fire and sword is no longer accepted, and it is now thought the transition was a far more complex one. The period often referred to as the Dark Ages saw the end of the pattern of life that had been established during the Roman occupation.

An ancient territorial boundary, known as the *Fullingadic*, ran southwards from the Thames at Weybridge at this time. The boundary probably related to the territory of the *Fullingas*, who might later be identified with the *Getinges*, an area in the occupation of *Geat* or his descendants. The Chertsey Abbey foundation charter seems to imply that land east of this boundary ditch, including the area which is now Cobham, had formerly been a part of Kent. The *Fullingadic* later formed a section of the ancient parish boundary where it runs from Redhill across Ockham Common.

10 *Leigh Hill* c.*1900. Pullen's Cottage can be seen on the right.*

11   *Eaton Grange. This house incorporates parts of the old Eaton Farm.*

Leigh Hill and Eaton Farm

During this period the settlement in the Leigh Hill area seems to have formed part of *Getinges*, and it is under this name that it was included in a Chertsey Abbey foundation grant of AD 675. There is some uncertainty as to whether *Getinges* applied only to Cobham or whether it included other places mentioned in the charter. However, it seems that *Getinges* was corrupted to 'Etynge in parochia de Coveham' by 1294 and in 1598 it was 'Yeatinge Fearme', now Eaton Grange, on the Eaton Park estate, which is a short distance from Leigh Hill on the Higher Terrace. 'Leigh' (or 'Lay' as it was still pronounced locally within living memory) probably meant a clearing in the woodland.

The seventh-century settlement probably consisted of between three and five halls or farmhouses with their ancillary farm buildings on the high ground overlooking the river. The settlement's cultivated arable land was beneath the hill in the area called the Tilt. A Saxon spear discovered at Leigh Hill in 1926 might indicate the site of a cemetery related to the settlement but no human or other remains were discovered at the time.

It was only in Saxon times that there were the real beginnings of any continuous community, the land being brought under till by the oxen-ploughs of peasants tied to the Abbey of St Peter at Chertsey both by allegiance and by payment of rents, fines and the provision of labour services. Erkenwald, later Bishop of London, had founded Chertsey Abbey in *c.*AD 666, under King Egbert of Kent. In the year 672, 'Frithuwold of the province of the men of Surrey, sub-king of Wulfhere king of Mercia' gave the estate at Cobham to the monastery as part of a foundation grant.

The name Surrey, or *Suthrige* as it was once known, appears to have been applied to the southern part of an area of Middle Saxon settlement of which Middlesex was the northern part. Under the later Saxon kings the county was divided into administrative units for defence and

12   *Sketch of a Saxon spear found at Leigh Hill in 1926.*

government called hundreds. Cobham fell within the Hundred of Elmbridge, which also included the parishes of Walton on Thames, Esher, Thames Ditton, East and West Molesey and Stoke D'Abernon. It is possible that the Hundred Court met in Cobham, and that the 'Elmbridge' name refers to the river crossing here, although East Molesey is also a contender for this important site.

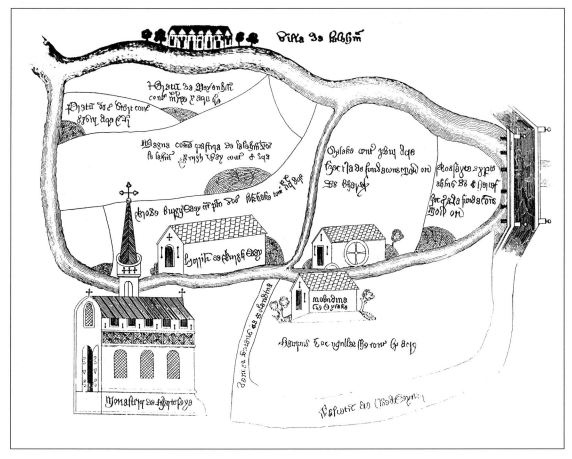

13   *A late 15th-century plan of Chertsey Abbey and its demesnes.*

Viking Raids

In the eighth and ninth centuries the kingdom of Wessex emerged as the major power, and ultimately the sole kingdom, south of the Thames. In AD 825 Surrey was permanently annexed to Wessex and this coincided with the first big Viking raid. In a later raid in AD 871 the Vikings sailed up the Thames attacking and plundering the settlements along the way. They arrived at Chertsey Abbey which they proceeded to sack, killing the abbot and ninety monks, burning buildings and laying waste the land. But it was not long before the Abbey was recolonised and became one of the largest and most influential monasteries in England. It was a major landholder in Surrey and an important influencing factor upon the estates in its possession such as Cobham. One of the most important and influential abbots was John de Rutherwyke, of whom more will be heard later.

Just eight miles from Cobham is the town of Kingston which, after Winchester, was one of the most important of all West Saxon towns. Several Saxon kings were crowned at Kingston between 900 and 979, the first being Edward the Elder, son of Alfred the Great, who had ended his reign as the first King of all England.

Domesday Book

In 1066 Duke William of Normandy conquered England and was crowned King. Most of the land of the English nobility was soon granted to his followers. The Anglo-Saxon Chronicle records how in 1085 in Gloucester the King, after 'deep speech with his counsellors', sent men all over England to each shire to find out what or how much each landholder held in land and livestock and what it was worth. The information was collected at Winchester and became Domesday Book. The whole undertaking was completed in less than a year.

The survey of Cobham is as follows:

> In ELMBRIDGE hundred
> The Abbey holds COBHAM itself. Before 1066 it answered for 30 hides, now for 12½ hides.
> Land for 10 ploughs. In lordship [Cobham Court Farm] 1 plough;
> 29 villagers and 6 cottagers with 9 ploughs
> 3 mills worth 13s 4d; meadow 1 acre; woodland worth 40 pigs
> Value before 1066 £20 now £14.
> William of Watteville holds 2 hides from the Abbey itself. An Englishman held them before 1066, and in King Edward's lifetime he gave this land to the church in alms. The land is in the manor of Esher.
> 6 villagers with 2 ploughs.
> Value before 1066 and now 14s 6d.

All monetary sums given are the annual values of rents and other manorial income. It is surprising to find such a small area of meadow for a riverside manor but this would have been important since it would be the only fenced grass land, and hence the only good hay land. 'Villagers' were those who held strips of land in the arable fields and 'Cottagers' were those who worked full time for the richer landowners. The land that was recorded as being in the manor of Esher is today known as Norwood Farm. The 40 pigs were due to the Abbey for the right to run seven to ten times that number in the woods where they could forage for acorns.

Because Cobham was in the hands of the Chertsey Abbey, an ecclesiastical corporation, it remained an Abbey possession rather than being handed to one of the King's Norman friends. Surrey was one of the more lightly settled areas of lowland England. The population figures recorded in Domesday Book are probably households and it has been suggested that a multiplier of four or five should be used to obtain some indication of the total population at this time. It is, however, possible that 'villager' means a typical villagers's holding and not necessarily a single family. A population of 140 - 175, if this can be assumed, is a substantial population but we do not know where they lived.

There is a strong probability that the present village of Church Cobham was laid out by the lord of the manor in the reign of King Stephen. It has been discovered that other Chertsey estates such as Egham were reorganised in the 12th century and it is quite possible that Cobham was planned at the same time.

The Market

An undated charter in the British Library relates to a Tuesday market at Cobham granted to the Abbot of Chertsey by King Stephen (1135-54). Stephen was well known for giving away lands, titles and royal rights to gain support for his tenuous grasp of the throne. The market may have been laid out at Street Cobham where the road from Church Cobham met the road from Kingston to Guildford. This would certainly account for the unusual width of the road at this point. Additionally, the 1870 Ordnance Survey map appears to show the last vestiges of a small green here. The market site might also have taken in land that now forms the little backwater of World's End. This would account for the old houses still to be found

14 *Street Cobham c.1820. This painting shows the bend in the old Portsmouth Road that may have been the site of the market granted by King Stephen. The building immediately behind the man on horseback was for many years a butcher's shop and the area to the left of it (now a development called The Chancery) was an area for keeping livestock and a slaughterhouse. (Private Collection)*

here and for the *Swan* inn that appears to have been in this area until the 18th century.

It is possible that an east-west route from Leatherhead through Cobham might predate the Portsmouth Road. If this were the case, the road to London would have formed a junction here, which could provide the reason for the unusual sharp bend that now exists.

A market such this would have provided a useful source of revenue to assist the financing of the creation of a settlement at Church Cobham, and it would be sensible for the market to be on the Guildford-Kingston road with its passing traffic rather than in the new settlement about half a mile to the south east. It would also be a major factor in the development of the separate community of Street Cobham. The market

15   *Church Street from an 1822 watercolour by John Hassell. (British Library)*

place would have been covered with booths and stalls for the different types of trader. Some stalls later became permanent. It is possible that a timber-framed house that once stood on the site now occupied by a modern development called The Chancery, and which was for many years Lynn's butcher's shop, may have been built alongside the market place. The market seems to have ceased by the end of the 16th century, by which time Street Cobham had developed into a roadside settlement with inns, alehouses, blacksmiths and all the other occupations that could benefit from the increasing traffic.

Church Street

Church Street was for centuries the 'spine' of Church Cobham and properties on the south side still occupy fairly ordered plots that could well date back to the 12th century. Perhaps the medieval occupants looked more to the river (water supply, or power for industry and fishing) than to agriculture. The rear boundaries of these house plots appear to follow the line of an earlier road, predating Church Street, that led from Cobham Court and Downside Bridge through to the Mill.

On the north side was Church Field, an open field where villagers had their strips of land. Church Field spread from Church Street towards Street Cobham and was crossed by lanes that have now become High Street and Between Streets. An old lane leading to Cobham Court and once called 'Court Way' still exists as a footpath running from the present High Street along Hollyhedge Road, crossing the new Downside Bridge Road. It acted as a boundary for the rear gardens of the properties that were later to be built on the north side of Church Street.

What is now the High Street remained largely undeveloped until the second quarter of the 19th century but an 1839 map of Cobham shows what appears to be a parallel

16 *Cobham Mill from an 1822 watercolour by John Hassell. (British Library)*

back lane on the east side which was lost when the Cedar Road schools (now Cobham Library) and Spencer Road were built. This could indicate an intention to lay out building plots here in medieval times. It seems likely that the original highway at this date continued on the opposite side of the present Church Street along Crown Alley, which is now a footpath linking the High Street to the Tilt. As late at the 18th century, properties overlooking the river had frontages that ran down to the water's edge with no public right of way. Another bridleway seems to have run along what is now Cedar Road giving access to the mill from Hogshill Lane. This might have provided an alternative thoroughfare to the present High Street.

Mills on the Mole

The steep gradient of the River Mole at Cobham, where it falls seven feet in half a mile, made this an excellent site for water mills. Domesday Book records three mills and these were probably at Cobham and Downside, on the site of the present mills, and at Ashford, where the 1845 Tithe Map shows a 'Mill Field' and a 'Mill Meadow'. In 1275 Abbot Bartholomew is recorded as having purchased one messuage and one mill and sixty acres of land called 'le Pypsyng' from Thomas Haunsard and Alice his wife. This is believed to have been at Ashford.

The Founding of the Church

Although no church is recorded at Cobham in Domesday Book, there may have been a small wooden building here used for public worship. When Chertsey Abbey acquired the estates recorded in its foundation charter it would have seen to it that each village had a chapel, although the abbot expected people to come to the Abbey on the principal feast days. This would eventually have led to the establishment of churches and the formation

17   *St Andrew's church from Cracklow's engraving of c.1820*

of various parishes, since the parish is usually the land that provides the tithe for the support of the parson. The present parish church of St Andrew dates from the middle of the 12th century and is first recorded in a Papal Bull of Alexander II in 1176. The original structure, no doubt built under the watchful eyes of the abbot and monks of Chertsey, consisted of a chancel, nave and tower. The church would have been the only stone building in the area and must have been an impressive sight surrounded by the simple wattle and daub houses of the villagers.

Whilst the abbots of Chertsey were necessarily concerned with the spiritual life of the area, raising revenue for the Abbey Church, and organising their dispersed estates into manageable communities, they also found time for sport and Henry I granted them the right to enclose whenever they wished an area near Downside Common (then known as 'Morelspark', or marshy

place) for hunting. At this time Cobham was part of Windsor Forest, and it paid the king to grant landowners the privilege of destroying animals harmful to beasts of the royal chase such as foxes, hares, pheasant and wild cats.

It was not until 1190 that the knights of Surrey offered Richard I 200 marks in order that 'they might be quit of all things that belong to the forest from the water of Wey to Kent and from the street of Guilford southwards as far as Surrey stretches'. After this time Windsor Forest came no closer to Cobham than Byfleet Bridge.

The King's Justice

Our knowledge of the lives of ordinary people at Cobham at this time is limited. However, we are fortunate to have a document that is the record of the Surrey Eyre of 1235, translated and published by the Surrey Record Society. The Eyre was a court held in the county by the King's Justices.

One item of local interest is the case of a Jewish lady named Antera, who was accidentally drowned in the river at Cobham. Antera owned two gold rings, a gold clasp and four shillings in money, which her brother Joce had absconded with. He was duly arrested, and since Antera was a Jewess the king was entitled to a third of her chattels. Presumably Antera had been fording the river, even though a bridge is said to have been built at the foot of Painshill by the saintly Queen Matilda, or Maud, wife of Henry I, in 1100 for the benefit of the soul of one of her maidens who was drowned here. The Queen assigned a plot of land on the Cobham side of the river to maintain half the bridge, while on the Walton side the lord of the manor

18 *Cobham Bridge from an 1823 watercolour by John Hassell. (British Library)*

gave a plot called 'Spitilcroft' for the upkeep of the other half. 'Spitil' is a corruption of hospital, and 'croft' indicates a small piece of arable land attached to the house, the whole meaning a little roadside resting place.

There was probably some sort of wooden bridge at Cobham long before the time of Henry I but when these flimsy structures fell into decay there was often a delay in carrying out repairs because it was difficult to get the land owners on each side to agree to their responsibilities. In 1350 it was reported that Cobham Bridge, built of stone and wood, was broken and ought to be repaired on its western part by the Earl of Hereford, but it was not until 1353 that Earl Humphrey repaired it. From the Eyre we also learn of a local case of suspected murder,

when 'A certain man ... lodged at the house of John Prodome with a horse, but he was never seen there afterwards; but the horse was found there.' The jury believed that John had murdered his unfortunate lodger and stolen his valuable horse. John's sentence was to be outlawed but we do not know the outcome. It is likely that it was a descendant of his, also named John, who held lands in Heywood in 1317. Heywood, now the site of the International Community School on the Fairmile, is said to have been 'a reputed manor' and a family named 'Heiwude' held land here in 1206.

A local name that is still in use today is mentioned in the case of John le Wallere and Alexander de Chilbrook, who were accused of larceny and associating with

19 *Heywood from a 19th-century engraving.*

thieves. This John le Wallere was probably related to the Ralph Wallere who owned property adjoining the parish church. The Chilbrook is a small stream that runs through the southern part of Cobham. It can be seen in a deep gully close to Halfpenny Cross. The Saxons called the gully *ceole*, or throat, and the stream became the 'ceole brook'. The name is also retained in Chilbrook Farm, an 18th-century building that stands nearby. In 1287 there was a lawsuit in Cobham concerning Peter de Kulsham and Godfrey le Leper and his wife Margery. Kulsham (or Culsham as it was also spelt) is possibly taken from the Welsh word *cil*, meaning 'back, corner or retreat', and may point to his having lived at the area now known as World's End, hidden area just off the main road at Street Cobham.

The surviving records of Chertsey Abbey begin to provide an insight into the lives of the more law-abiding citizens of Cobham at this time through various property transactions handled by the manor courts in the 14th and 15th centuries. Surnames were rare and villagers were usually named after either their occupation or where they lived. In 1294 we hear of Robert atte Lye (Leigh Hill) and William atte Kneppe (Knipp Hill), and in 1239 it was recorded that Abraham the bridge keeper at Cobham 'had long lived there'.

Four

CHURCH AND MANOR

The two most important influences upon the people who lived in Cobham in the early Middle Ages were those of the Manor and the Church and the authority of the latter was central to medieval society: 'It set out the calendar for the year in work, prayer and festivals. It laid down normal rules of behaviour and set out the goals of life.'

St Andrew's church

About fifty years after its founding, Cobham church was enlarged and the chancel extended eastwards, the whole being set at a slight angle to the nave. It has been suggested this was to represent the droop of Christ's head on the cross, or to capture the orientation of the sunrise on the festival of

20   *St Andrew's church from a 19th-century drawing.*

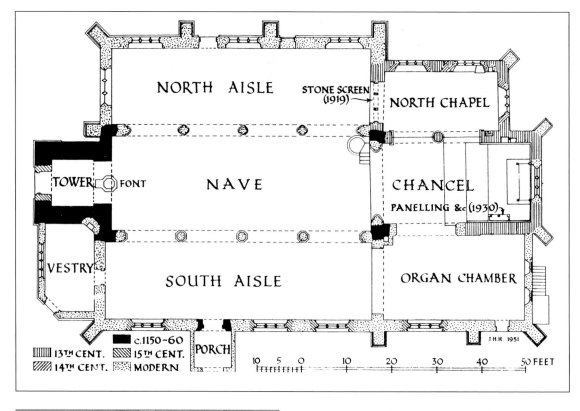

21   *Plan of St Andrew's church.*

22   *The Norman south doorway at St Andrew's church, from an 1827 watercolour by E. Hassell. (British Library)*

St Andrew. A chapel was also added on the north side. This was originally nearly double its present length and the outline of one of the original early English lancet windows can still be seen on the outside wall. Inside the chapel the original triangular-headed double piscine with its two shallow basins and soakaways is still in the south wall. This was used for cleansing the sacred vessels after mass and probably dates from the time of Edward I. It is tempting to imagine that Edward himself may have prayed in St Andrew's during visits he made to Cobham. When the chapel floor was taken up in the 19th century, several pieces of old tombstone were found, including fragments of a slab thought to be contemporary with the chapel.

Although drastically restored and enlarged in the 19th century, the church retains one of the finest Norman doorways in Surrey. Its elaborate design is of three rows of chevron and billet mouldings with a detached shaft on each side of its outer face. Fortunately the Victorian restorers had the sense to save the doorway and move it to its present position when the south aisle was added to the church in 1854. It has been used as the main entrance to the church for nearly nine hundred years, and through it have passed many interesting and colourful personalities.

The impressive tower appears to be contemporary with the south porch, although it might be just a few years older. It is square in plan and contains two floors. The tower walls are three and a half feet thick and built of rubble, pudding stone and flint. Incredible though it may seem, the tower is built on sand without any foundation. The interior of the tower has a fine Norman arch although it is much plainer that the south doorway arch. The only ornamentation is on the pier capitals. The deep grooves that can be seen in the arch overhead are something of a mystery and seem to have been created by the bell ropes being pulled from inside the nave and rubbing against the stonework. Perhaps there was once neither steeple nor roof and the bell ringers had a damp job in bad weather.

Rectors and Vicars

Although Chertsey Abbey appears to have received papal permission to appoint vicars in about 1190, it continued to appoint rectors until 1465. The original rectory seems to have been to the south east of the church on the site now occupied by 'Rose Lodge'. The

23 & 24 *Church Stile House (left) from a postcard of c.1900. The brass (right) is of an unknown priest in vestments.*

earliest known rector of Cobham was Aymer de Fureth, who was appointed by Aymer, Abbot of Chertsey, in *c.*1166. The early rectors and, later, the vicars seem to have been men of some substance and learning. Rectories were often used as a means of supporting clergy whose main employment was in royal or ecclesiastical administration. They would appoint assistants, often called parish chaplains, to be the resident priests. Aymer de Fureth's successor, Adam de Ivelcestre (Ilchester), became Dean of Salisbury in 1215. He was the dean who called together the canons to consult regarding the removal of the see of Salisbury from Old Sarum to its present site.

In 1218 the churchyard was extended to the road on the west as part of a settlement of a tithe dispute between Adam, Abbot of Chertsey, and Adam de Ivelcestre, who was then both rector of Cobham and Dean of Salisbury. The newly acquired ground, opposite the house now called Pyports, had been occupied by some houses belonging to a man called Ralph Wallere.

The vicar of Cobham seems to have lived at this time in a property on the site of the present Church Stile House in Church Street. Alan, Abbot of Chertsey (1223-61), paid 20 shillings in silver for a property on this site that was at the time let to Henry, vicar of Cobham, by a person called Payn Urry. It consisted of a house and adjoining garden and 'all appurtenances containing half an acre and ten feet of water and land'. When in later years, vicars were appointed, they lived at the house that later became known as Woodend and is now the site of Woodend Park, off Stoke Road. A 15th-century brass of an unknown priest in

vestments, holding a chalice and host, can be seen in the church.

Although the prime use of the parish church was for services on Sundays and feast days, the villagers also gathered there for community activities and merry making. Sometimes the church even served as a market place. In the Middle Ages most people stood in church, although the elderly and infirm might 'go the wall' and sit on a bench. Following the introduction of pews, space for meetings and communal gatherings was restricted. This led to the building of 'Church Houses', which were used for meetings of the Vestry and for social events such as 'Church Ales'. A building which adjoined the churchyard at Cobham, and was called 'Church House', may have served this purpose. The property was largely rebuilt in the 18th century and is now called 'Church Cottage'.

The Manors

For centuries local administration and land ownership were largely in the hands of the manorial lords. The old parish of Cobham contained the lands of the manors of Cobham, Ham, Down (reputed), Heywood (reputed), Esher Episcopi and Esher Milbourne. The chief manor was that of Cobham, which was owned by Chertsey Abbey. The Abbey employed a bailiff to oversee the day-to-day management of the Manor. A large number of the early records of the Abbey have survived and been published as the Chertsey Cartulary and they provide a valuable insight into the administration of the manor at this time.

The manors were controlled by courts presided over by the lord's bailiff assisted by

25 *Downside Farm. The present property dates largely from the 18th century but probably stands on the site of the original Downe Hall or Place.*

a jury of tenants. The Court Baron dealt with land transactions, and the Court Leet with minor offences committed on the manor. An important right of the manor was the 'View of Frankpledge', a court to which the men of the three tithings of Church Cobham, Street Cobham and Downside were separately responsible for misdeeds committed among themselves. Manorial constables were also appointed to help keep the peace.

The Manor of Downe

Although no records seem to have survived for the manor of Downe, it was always the most important private estate in the parish and seems to take its name from the hill or down which can be seen rising steeply from the river within the present Cobham Park. Recent research by Margaret Gelling, an expert on place-names, has shown that the word 'Dun' or 'Dune' is commonly used in settlement-names for low hills which provide good settlement-sites, usually in areas of relatively low relief'. This description perfectly fits the site at Cobham Park. Gelling also says that the name is usually given to an ancient settlement site which pre-dates Anglo-Saxon times: 'the element dune is a name which would convey to an Anglo-Saxon both the nature of the site and the likelihood of the settlement being a high status one.' It therefore seems possible that the site in Cobham Park could be quite ancient and worthy of closer examination.

A man called Deodatus de Dunes held land in Cobham in the reign of King John and presumably lived in a property either within, or close to the present Cobham Park.

26 & **27**   *Cobham Court (left) from an 1822 watercolour by John Hassell (British Library). The brass (right) in St Andrew's church is believed to represent James Sutton, Bailiff of the Manor of Cobham, who died in 1530.*

Recent research clearly points to the manor house, known as Downe Hall or Place, as having stood on the site of the present Downside Farm, and the curved water feature that can still be seen here is possibly the remains of an early moat. The moat would have been a means of emphasising the social standing of the house and its occupants.

In the 13th and 14th centuries William de la Dune held the royal office of Keeper of the Hanaper. The hanaper was a basket made to hold the royal seal, and state documents appear to indicate that Edward I stayed at Downe Place at various dates between 1292 and 1306. When William de Doune died, in 1331, his son Henry took his place on payment to Chertsey Abbey of an ox valued at 13s. 4d. He was also required to pay a sum of 15s. 9d. and give nine gallons of honey and a horse. The honey was annual payment to the Abbey for allowing Doune's tenants to grind corn at Downside mill. In 1386-7 Henry Doune was involved in legal transactions with his neighbour Thomas Freke who lived at Chasemore Farm.

By the 15th century the name Dune or Doune had become Downe, and in 1449-50 John a Downe, 'King's Servant', who was probably related to the Cobham family, was Member of Parliament for Guildford. The Manor of Downe seems to have merged with that of Cobham in the 18th century.

Cobham Court

The house from which the manor of Cobham was administered was Cobham Court, which still stands although much altered over the centuries. In 1331 Abbot John de Rutherwyck (1307-46) repaired the 'Chamber at Cobham' and added a new chapel to the house. Until the dissolution of the Abbey, a bailiff would have managed the manor from this building, assisted by a rent collector. A brass in St Andrew's church of a man in armour is believed to be that of James Sutton, 'bayle of this lordshyppe', who died in 1530, his son Richard appears to have been the last bailiff.

Abbot John was responsible for a determined campaign of improvement and acquisition designed to bolster the Abbey's then failing revenues. He was described as 'the convent's second founder … and the substantial improver of the manors belonging to the Monastery'. He rebuilt the mills at Cobham and Ashford and constructed a new mill house which probably stood on the site of the Old Mill House, opposite Cobham Mill. The Surrey Domestic Buildings Research Group has dated the Old Mill House to the 16th century, which makes it one of the oldest surviving buildings in Cobham, and it may well incorporate some of the fabric of the house constructed by Abbot John. Abbot John's attempts to increase the Abbey's revenues brought about a certain amount of public hostility and a document of 1334 in the Public Record Office deals with the claims of certain Cobham men that he had been indulging in rent raising and other questionable means of enlarging the Abbey's coffers.

Timber was an important and much valued asset of the manor and in 1314-15 Osberte de Ponte was accused at Westminster of cutting down an oak at Cobham that was the property of the Abbot of Chertsey. In Cobham the lord of the manor had the right to receive fines for releasing stray animals from the Pound, a wooden-fenced enclosure which in early times stood by what is now Cobham Park, opposite the end of Plough Lane. In more recent times the Pound was on the green by the entrance to Cobham Court near Downside Bridge. The manorial court elected the pinder or pound keeper. The lord also had the right to 'waif', or abandoned property, and 'pannage', the revenue from his tenants' pigs on the common.

28   *The Conventual Seal of Chertsey Abbey.*

Fourteenth-century People

A taxation document of 1332 provides us with one of the first lists of Cobham people. Many of the names incorporated their place of residence, and some we can still identify with local properties today, such as Laurence Cosyn (Cossins), William le Pypard (Pyports), Robert de Pontyngton (Pointers), Osbert Hamond of Yettynge (Eaton Farm), William ate Brok (Brook Farm), John ate Knep (Knipp Hill), Philip ate Hoke, next la Tilthe (Hook Farm, Cobham Tilt), Richard ate Mersshe (Marsh Place, now Chestnut Lodge, by the Old Common), and Peter Dogel, the smith at Longboyelands (Longboyds, Church Street). We also hear of Dodewyck, which means Dudda's 'wic' or dairy farm (now Chasemore Farm, Downside).

The poorest villagers lived in small single-storey cottages constructed from wattle and daub with thatched roofs and unglazed windows protected by wooden shutters. Those slightly better off might have had a house of two bays with one floored over to create a service room with a solar or bedroom above it, the other open to the roof, creating a hall with an open hearth. Buildings would have been constructed from local material and the woods around the village were plentiful in oak and chestnut. (Oak trees from nearby Stoke D'Abernon were used in the construction of the magnificent roof at Westminster Hall in London.) No doubt the marshy areas around the river Mole would have provided reeds for the lath and plaster walls.

Plots for building were granted by the lord of the manor, and in 1329-30 Gilbert le Bolk was admitted to a plot of land next to the churchyard stile, fourteen feet long to the west of the stile along the churchyard wall, by eight feet wide, with permission to build. This appears to have been opposite the house called 'Overbye' in Church Street. A plot of this size is incredibly small, even for a cottage, and so there is some uncertainty as to what Gilbert was planning to build here. In fact no evidence of actual building on the site has been found and presumably it now forms parts of the present churchyard.

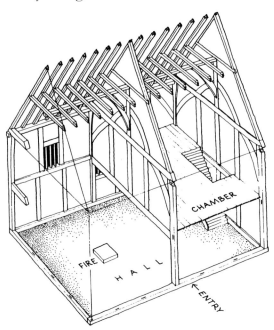

29   *Drawing of a simple two-storey timber-framed house. The hall occupies two bays, but one of these is floored over to provide an upper room or solar in that half.*

The Open Fields

The tenants' land holdings were in the open fields, where each person's holding was divided into long thin strips called 'selions'. In this way a man's land might be spread out all over the manor. Despite its obvious drawbacks, it did ensure that everyone had a fair share of both good and bad land.

30   *Cobham Tilt from a postcard of c.1910.*

Cultivation of the fields was on a communal basis with an agreed cycle of crop rotation and fallow grazing.

It was the large Church Field that kept the communities of Street Cobham and Church Cobham apart for many centuries. A survey of the Manor of Cobham made by Ralph Agas in 1598 provides us with the names of the common fields. These were North Field, Church Field, Appleton Field, West Croft, Down Field, Puntington Field and Rewoorthe. Church Field lay between the church, Street Cobham and Hogshill. It was divided into 12 furlongs with names such as Anyards, Mill Furlong, Church Furlong, Little Ham and Hamwell. The modern name of Anvil Lane is a corruption of Hamwell, by which name it was known until well into the 19th century. Appleton Field lay to the south and east of Leigh Hill, and Down Field was probably within what is now Cobham Park. Puntington Field was behind the Black Swan at Hatchford and Rewoorthe was close by.

Common Fields and Common Rights

Manorial tenants also had the right to graze cattle on the extensive wastes or commons such as the Old Common and the Tilt. The Tilt was originally a much larger area and, although once arable land, by the 13th century it had become pasture, meadow and wood. The change of use might have been due to newly created or rearranged open fields being established around the settlement of Church Cobham. In 1268-9 an agreement was made between John Medmenham, Abbot of Chertsey, and Sir John d'Abernon, lord of the neighbouring manor, by which the latter's tenants were allowed to make use of the Tilt Common at certain times of the year. Pigs found good forage in the woodland between Cobham and Esher which was reached by the aptly named Hogshill Lane. Downside Road was formerly known as Poultry Lane, possibly indicating some connection with a different form of livestock. An area known as Goose Green which, before the construction of the M25, existed on the edge of Downside Common may have been for the grazing of geese by tenants of the manor of Downe.

One of the ancient privileges of the Manor of Cobham was that of holding a fair on the feast of St Andrew. The fair was for cows, steers, horses, sheep and pigs and was held until 1859 in a field at Street Cobham, on the site now occupied by a house called Faircroft. It is likely it had been held earlier in the sharp bend of the old Portsmouth Road, outside the former *White Lion* inn, where it is suggested the former Tuesday market had been held. In 1796 a meadow near Downside Bridge known as Fair Meadow may have been the original site of the fair. The River Mole was crucial to the people in the 14th century as it provided the power to drive the wheels of the three mills as well as the water needed for the tannery which once stood on the site of Cedar House.

The Black Death

A rapidly increasing population and intensive use of land were hallmarks of this time. However, all this came to a dramatic end when the Black Death appeared in 1348 and swept away about a third of the population of Europe. Conditions for the peasants had been declining for some time following a series of droughts, floods, storms and bad summers. When the Black Death struck the people had little resistance to it and many of the village families died out altogether. The plague moved along the trade routes. In England it travelled from Southampton across Hampshire and Surrey towards London. Farnham, just 20 miles from Cobham, was severely hit by the plague, as was Banstead, which is only a few miles in the opposite direction. At nearby Esher all the brothers at Sandon Priory died as a result of the Black Death. To avert the divine wrath the Bishop of Winchester instructed his clergy to exhort their flocks to attend the sacrament of penance and process barefoot with heads bowed around the market place or through the churchyard reciting the greater litany.

It may be that Cobham avoided the worse ravages of the Black Death for on 7 March 1349, at the height of the plague, William Edington, Bishop of Winchester, made his recorded visit here. He chose Cobham to ordain an abnormally large number of clerics, many of whom were to replace those who had died. The fact he chose to make his visit at this time seems to indicate he believed Cobham a relatively safe place.

Five

THE END OF THE OLD ORDER

The Effects of the Black Death

Recovery from the effect of the Black Death was slow, especially as the plague continued sporadically for the next twenty years. We can only imagine the effect this had on villagers of Cobham. Buildings that had been occupied by those who had died of the plague were burnt to the ground. Their associated land holdings were often allowed to revert to waste or common, thereby turning back the clock on much of the progress made during the preceding century as the community had established itself. However, the Black Death ultimately accelerated economic and social change and increased individual wealth.

Where vacant holdings did not revert back to waste, tenants found themselves able to rent land for a cash payment instead of being tied by various feudal services to the lord of the manor. In 1379 Peter ate Mershe of Cobham, who had previously been obliged to provide the Abbot of Chertsey with 'one horse fit for the monarch to ride on and also to ride himself with the King whenever and wherever he is ordered and to come with one man each autumn to reap corn on the manor farm', had his rent commuted to 4s. in lieu of these services. Agreements of this sort resulted in many of the old ties being broken and a new class emerging known as 'copyholders', who held their land by a written copy of the entry of the transaction in the manorial court rolls. Properties began to be referred to by the name of the copyholder and were passed down from one generation to the next. Cobham possesses a good set of Court Rolls which run right down to modern times and through them it is possible to trace the history of many of our older houses.

Taxation and Revolt

Hard on the heels of the Black Death, the people were subject to another hardship in the shape of a Poll Tax levied upon every householder. A series of taxes was imposed both to finance the war with France and to compensate for government mismanagement. Things came to a head in 1380 when the third such tax in four years was levied. The following year Wat Tyler led his famous rebellion and, on 12 June 1381, rebels in Surrey and Sussex joined forces and marched to Southwark, where they broke open the Marshalsea and King's Bench prisons. After a face-to-face meeting with Richard II, Tyler was killed and his head cut off and displayed on London Bridge. However, trouble was still rife in the countryside and, locally, Guildford was attacked and records were destroyed.

31   *A medieval open hall house.*

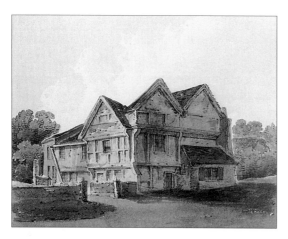

32   *Church Stile House. The present building dates from the 17th century but incorporates parts of an earlier building.*

Chertsey Abbey tenants also rioted, burning some of the manorial rolls.

In addition to the plague and taxation, in 1352, the people of Cobham were further burdened by an order which granted the keeper of the King's stud at Guildford together with the keeper of the King's carts and sumpter horses and the Queen's averner, the right of compulsory purchase in the village as well as in several other places in Surrey.

The Black Death resulted in fewer tenants and there was therefore more land to go round. Richer peasants started to live in better houses, some of which have survived until today. The economy of the village at this time depended chiefly upon arable farming and the rearing and grazing of animals on the meadowland adjacent to the river and on the extensive commons around Cobham, the so-called 'manorial waste' on which cattle, certain types of horses and ponies, geese and often sheep were grazed. Enclosed pastures were used for grazing the more valuable livestock such as oxen and better quality horses. Meadows, especially in well-watered situations, were grazed at certain times of the year, but livestock was excluded to allow the grass to grow for the hay crop. Also, of course, the common arable fields were thrown open for common grazing after harvest and during periods of fallow.

The Development of Timber-Framed Houses in the Village

Surrey is rich in medieval hall houses rebuilt at this time. They were constructed with timber framing which was made up in the local carpenter's shop and then taken to the site to be assembled. The smaller cottages often only had a hall of one bay that was open to the roof, or with one end floored over and reached by a ladder. The larger houses of the better-off farmers were built of good quality material and often embellished with carvings and mouldings. The best end of the house, with its solar bedroom, was furthest away from the service end and entrance. The room under the solar was used as a parlour or as a second bedroom. The exterior timber framing was either left in its natural colour or painted with red ochre as a preservative. The infill panels were made from wattle and daub, which consisted of upright oak staves woven with hazel rods. These were then covered with a thick layer of daub made by mixing mud with cow dung and horsehair.

At this time only churches and great houses had glass and ordinary houses had either wooden shutters or, sometimes, oiled silk or linen to allow some light to penetrate the dark interior. An open hearth in the centre of the hall heated the house and the smoke was left to find its way out through the thatched roof or through specially constructed louvres. The smells from cooking and the smoke must have made living conditions very unpleasant during the winter months. In later years detached kitchens were sometimes built away from the house to avoid the fire risk. Still later, smoke bays were developed and then brick hearths were inserted into these. Finally chimneys were built using bricks when they became more readily available in the 16th century, although smoke bays also continued to be used into this period.

33   *La Capanna. Now a restaurant, the central part of this property is an open hall house.*

34   *Chasemore Farm, Bookham Common Road. The present 18th-century house stands on the site of an earlier property known as 'Dudwickes', the property of the Freke family in the 14th and 15th centuries.*

Cobham still has several buildings which, although altered over the centuries, date from medieval times. These include Cedar House, Pyports, Church Stile House and Old Cottage on the edge of Oxshott Heath, a former warrener's lodge. The core of what is now 'La Capanna' in the High Street is a medieval hall house.

Some Cobham Families

Documentary evidence for this period is scant but we do know a little of the lives of some of the more wealthy members of the community, such as the Freke family of Dudwicke's (now Chasemore Farm). The Freke family were living there in 1395-6 and Thomas Freke, who died in 1415, described

35 *Cobham Vicarage from an 1822 watercolour by John Hassell. This house stood on Cobham Tilt on the site now occupied by Woodend Park. This became the site of the vicarage in 1717. (Surrey History Service)*

himself in his will as citizen and 'woodmonger' of London. He desired to be buried in the churchyard of St Andrew by Baynards Castle, London (rebuilt after the Great Fire as St Andrew by the Wardrobe), where he probably had a wharf for landing his timber. Freke also left a legacy to the poor of St Andrew's, Cobham, and the sum of two shillings for repairing Downside Bridge.

In 1465 the Chertsey Cartulary stated Thomas Parys had held of the Abbey one messuage and one virgate of land called 'Cosyns', which had then been granted to John Sterre of Cobham who was to maintain two houses on the property. 'Cosyns' (now Cossins) is a residential care home on the Downside Road and the earliest parts of the present house date from the middle of the 18th century. It is possible the neighbouring property, now known as Park Farmhouse, was the other house maintained by John Sterre although the present house here dates from the late 16th century.

It is in the 15th century that we have the earliest record of one of the first of the many inns that were opened on the road to Guildford. In 1431 Chertsey Abbey granted the *Swan* at Street Cobham to James Godhelpe. The actual site of the *Swan* is a mystery despite the fact that it survived as an inn well into the 18th century.

The Vicarage

In 1465 Chertsey Abbey appropriated the Rectory and founded the Vicarage of Cobham. The Vicarage was endowed with the rectory house and garden, the barns excepted, and an annual sum of 14 marks. From this time until 1717 most of the vicars seemed to live to the south of the church, probably on the site of the rectory now occupied by Rose Lodge. In 1593 the churchwardens paid 8s. 4d. for mending the 'the vickeryge house', and in 1631 we learn that the church 'paynes' (lengths of churchyard fencing) began at the 'vicaridge gate'.

Six

The Tudors

Local Administration

The divorce of Henry VIII and Catherine of Aragon and the split with Rome led to the dissolution of most of the large monastic houses and their estates. These institutions had owned and controlled vast areas of the country for many centuries. In 1537 all this came to an end.

Since at least the seventh century, Cobham had been under the control of the Abbots of Chertsey. One of the last bailiffs was Richard Sutton. The last rent collector appears to have been John Charleton, collector of Bookham and Cobham. In 1534 the Abbot of Chertsey granted a 40 years' lease of the manor of Cobham to Richard Sutton's son, James, and three years later the lease passed to the Crown. Richard seems to have had four sons, Edmund, John, James and Jasper, and when he died their mother, Elizabeth, married George Bigley, who then became bailiff for the Crown.

After the death of Henry VIII, the Bigleys purchased the manor of Cobham from his daughter, Queen Mary, for the sum of £1,092 14s. The purchase included Cobham Court Farm, Church House and Cobham Mill. Bigley died in 1558 and the manor eventually passed to the Gavell family. In 1572 Robert Gavell received a grant of arms.

Hampton Court Chase

Two years after the dissolution of Chertsey Abbey, an Act of Parliament was passed creating the Honour of Hampton Court. Henry had acquired the manor of Hampton Court from Cardinal Wolsey and set about

36 *The Adoration of the Shepherds (top) c.1500. This unique Tudor representation of the birth of Christ was probably once part of a larger brass. A lost brass from Cobham church (bottom) showing a group of 15 sons may originally have been part of the nativity brass.*

37 *Cobham Court, c.1865*

rebuilding the palace on a grand scale. The King needed a suitable park and hunting ground and his officials, either by purchase or exchange, acquired large areas of land in this part of Surrey including Cobham. An 'honour' was the technical name for a group of manors and a chase was for the hunting of game – mainly deer.

The Chase was enclosed by a fence and dry ditch that was, in parts, five and half feet broad and four feet deep. The exact route of the fence is difficult to determine but, from its beginning opposite Hampton Court, it probably passed near the site of Claremont, then across Fairmile Common to the Mole below Ashford. It would have touched the original Cobham Park and then crossed the

38 *Henry VIII.*

39   *Cedar House. The tannery which stood here in the medieval period may have provided hair for the plaster that covered the walls of Oatlands Palace.*

Wey above Wisley church to join up with the south-west corner of Byfleet Park. The connection was made with the south-east corner of Woking Park. There were six 'sawtrees' or deerleaps in the fence so constructed that deer could enter the Chase but not escape. Gates were constructed for horses and carts to pass through and there were stiles for those on foot. Some of the timber for the fence was cut in Cobham and a postern gate was constructed at 'Cobham Fold', which was probably on the Fairmile Common. Forest law prevailed within the chase. Freeholders might cut down timber without licence and they could also fence or hedge in areas for growing corn, but once the corn had been cut and carried away then the King's officers could remove the edges and fences or make deer leaps. Freeholders had a reduction in rent and the fine levied upon copyholders inheriting upon death was

halved but, needless to say, the whole exercise was greatly resented by local people, who were put to considerable hardship. The fence was removed after the King's death, but the area is still technically a royal chase and subject to all former laws.

In addition to rebuilding and enlarging Hampton Court, Henry VIII also built a new palace within the Chase, Oatlands Palace at nearby Weybridge, the construction of which began in 1538. Of this magnificent structure nothing remains save for a few sections of the foundations. No doubt the building of Oatlands provided employment for local people and we know from the surviving accounts that James Bygnall, a tanner from Cobham, was among those who provided quantities of animal hair which was required to be mixed with the plaster that would cover the walls of the new palace. Bygnall's tannery may have been on the site of Cedar House since this building was still referred to in the 17th century as the 'tan house'. This would have been an ideal site and the fact that, in 1609 and 1652, Charles Collyns and Francis Sutton respectively were local tanners seems to indicate that it may have existed here for many years.

A Manorial Survey

In 1546-9 William Goodwyn made an extensive survey of the manor which records the names of all the freeholders and tenants of the manor together with their various holdings. Sadly, the map appears to have been lost and it is only possible to identify a few of the properties. One interesting name that occurs is that of 'William Lylly' who may have been an ancestor of William Lilly, the famous astrologer, who lived in Walton-on-Thames in the 17th century. Lilly is said to have foretold the Great Plague of 1665 and the Fire of London in 1666. The survey records that, 'George Bigley holds in the right of Elizabeth his wife, late the wife of Richard Sutton, one messuage with a garden adjoining in Street Cobham, abutting to the east upon land of William Lylly, and towards the west upon a certain land there, towards the north upon the common field called Northefield, and towards the south upon the king's way there.' Presumably Lilly's land was somewhere close to the River Mole and the parish boundary with Walton.

The survey also records a family who became better known in Cobham in the 18th century, that of 'John Frelond of Brownes'. 'Brownes' was in the neighbouring parish of

40   *Downside Bridge. This postcard shows the 18th-century bridge that was destroyed in the severe floods of 1968.*

41   *A 19th-century view of Cobham Mill.*

Ockham, where the Freelands had lived since at least the 14th century. John Freeland held four acres in the common field called 'Poytonfeld' in the southern part of Cobham parish. It was another John Freeland who, in the middle of the 18th century, was to purchase Pyports, a large old house that still stands opposite St Andrew's church.

William Wren held copyhold land at 'Yettyng called Kneppys'. 'Yettyng' is now Eaton Park and 'Kneppys' is Knipp Hill. George Bygley held 'one cottage with a yard in Cobham to the south of the churchyard of the parish church there', and this was probably on the site of the property now called Church Cottage. John Bignold held 'Brokeland and Niklyng' which later became the site of a house called Brooklands in Fairmile Lane and of Knowle Hill, between Fairmile Lane and the boundary with Stoke D'Abernon parish). In 1528 John Bygnold

of Cobham left 20d. 'to making the down bridge' (Downside Bridge) and 20d. 'to mending poultry alon' (Downside Road). This was probably John Bignold of Brooklands, Cobham, an ancestor of Sir Charles Robert Bignold, Lord Mayor of Norwich in 1926-7 and founder of the Norwich Union Insurance Company.

In 1552 Edward VI demised Cobham Mill to Sir Anthony Browne for 21 years on the condition that he should keep in repair the 'Cogges, Ronges, and les Bayes of the said Mill'. Later that year George Bygley, servant to Sir Anthony, demised the mill to Thomas Howse. Twenty years later, Robert and Dorothy Gavell, son-in-law and daughter of George Bygley, demised Cobham Mill to William Sewer of Fetcham for a term of 21 years. The premises were described as one corn mill and one malt mill, 'being under one rofe'.

Crime and Punishment

Witchcraft, robbery, murder and sexual scandal were not unknown to the people of Cobham at this time. In 1565, at Croydon Assizes, Joan Gowse of Cobham was sentenced to a year's imprisonment for bewitching to death an ox belonging to James Adowne. Adowne was probably a member of the family who lived at Down Place (now Cobham Park). The outcome of the trial is not known. Three years later, in 1568, Elizabeth Colpitt was found guilty of murdering her illegitimate daughter in the house of William Stone, a Cobham innholder. Colpitt had put her infant daughter into a sawpit near the house and smothered her with sawdust.

A crime of a different sort occurred in 1577 when five men attacked Jasper Swyfte and his servant 'in the highway at Cobham' and stole his horse, together with articles of gold and money. In 1581 three men 'apprehended for piracies' were sent from Arundel to London to stand trial. It was the job of the local constables and tithing men of the villages along their route to be responsible for their secure custody. Unfortunately, two of the pirates made a successful bid for freedom in the woods between Horsley and Cobham and the constables and tithing men were called to account for allowing their escape.

In 1572 a young woman called Judith Parvys found herself pregnant. She claimed that William Collyns, who worked at the *George Inn* at Street Cobham, was the father of the child she was carrying. However, William Hall, the innkeeper, swore on oath that Collyns told him, 'As God shall judge me I rid no further in the cart with her, but from Shorter's door to Best's house, which as this deponent sayeth is almost three quarters of mile.' It seems that Shorter, another innkeeper, then came under suspicion for Judith's condition and that he then bribed a woman named Elizabeth to say, 'that she had seen the said Judith playing the whore with one William an ostler of the George at Cobham'.

A scandal of a totally different sort occurred in 1586. Cobham has a long and continuous tradition of nonconformity, and in 1586 'Joan Lyster of Cobham Spinster' was indicted for using 'scandalous words' when she publicly said, 'the Bysshop of Canterbury and the Counsayle make fool of the Queens Majestie, and because she is but a woman she ought not to be governer of a Realme. And that the bishop of Canterbury was but a preest, and that the world would change erre it were longe.' Presumably Joan was the sister of George Lyster, the vicar of Cobham who, in 1578, had been indicted for 'failing to wear the surplice during divine service', a clear statement of his Puritanism.

Elizabeth I visits Cobham

In 1590 the woman Joan Lyster had said ought not to be a 'governer of a Realme' passed through Cobham on a royal progress and gave the village bell ringers a good excuse for a party, even though ringing for royalty was a statutory obligation. The Church-wardens' Book contains the following record of Queen Elizabeth I's visit to Mr Lyfield's house at Stoke D'Abernon:

Itm layd out to Stydall his wife
For bread and drink sett out for the Ringers
When the Queen went through the

42   *Pullen's Cottage, Leigh Hill. Once known as 'Tyrell's Croft', this is a 'smoke bay' house dating from* c.*1580.*

Towne from Mr Lyfelds howse . . . . vijd.
Itm payd to the Ringers that did
Ring when the Queene went through
The town from Mr Lyfields howse . . . . xd.

Ralph Agas's Survey

Eight years after the Queen's visit another survey of the manor was carried out. This time the surveyor was Ralph Agas. Like the Walwyn survey, the Agas survey has no map. This is a great pity since Agas is well known for his maps of Oxford, Cambridge and London. Agas's survey, undertaken for Francis Gavell, is much more detailed than Walwyn's and gives the name, area, boundaries and ownership of most of the enclosures in the manor. In what appears to be an unfinished survey there are many local place-names that can still be recognised today. These include 'Yeatinge Fearme' (now Eaton Grange), 'Chatley' (now Chatley Farm), 'Chilbrookes' (now Chilbrook Farm), and 'Great Hogges Hill' (Hogshill Lane). 'Somers' and 'Christmas' were two adjoining properties that stood on the site now occupied by Lime House in Church Street.

The Churchwardens' Book

Another important document from this time is the Churchwardens' Book that dates from 1588. This provides details of many of the matters relating to the administration of parish life and maintenance of St Andrew's church. In it we find the names of the ordinary families who were living in Cobham. There were regular payments made to many of the poorer people in the parish as well as to maimed soldiers and prisoners in the White Lion prison at Southwark.

In 1598 the churchwardens purchased a spade at 'St Andrew's fair'. In 1630 there were problems with dampness in the church and the sum of 2s. 11d. was paid out for 'masons work & stuff to mend certain dripps & other little things'. A more unusual item recorded in the Churchwardens' Book in 1593 is the sum of 3s. 4d. 'paid to the beaken kepinge'. The beacon was not necessarily in Cobham but may have served several parishes and there was certainly one in neighbouring West Horsley. It was part of a unique early warning system to warn of invasion or other threat to national security. Another reminder of the fear of invasion by the Spanish at this time is a muster of armed horsemen within the County of Surrey that was held at Cobham in the same year.

'The Great Rebuilding'

The appearance of Cobham began to change dramatically at about this time, as innovative methods were used in house construction. Medieval houses, with their smoky open halls, were being replaced by a style known as 'smoke bay houses'. In these properties the fire was moved to one end of the house and a partition constructed from the first-floor level to the roof up which the smoke would be drawn. Two examples of this type of house are *Pullens Cottage*, at the foot of Leigh Hill (*c.*1580), which was once known as 'Tyrells Croft', and *Plough Corner Cottage* on the Downside Road (*c.*1600).

Whilst the smoke bay was adopted by the less wealthy, the emerging yeoman farmers made use of the increasing

43 *Plough Corner Cottage, a 'smoke bay' house dating from about 1600.*

44   *A 19th-century engraving of Park Farm House, Downside Road. This timber-framed house was built at the end of the 16th century. It is of a type known as a 'central chimney stack' house.*

45   *The* White Lion *inn. The 18th-century red-brick façade hides an older structure dating from the 16th century.*

availability of locally produced bricks to construct chimneys. A brick chimney was far safer than a wattle and daub smoke bay. Sometimes brick chimneys were built at the end of an existing house, but towards the end of the 16th century a new style of building was introduced which is called the 'central chimney stack house'. A good local example of this style is to be found at 'Park Farmhouse' on the Downside Road. This has a central brick built chimney and was entered by a centrally placed front door opposite the side of the chimney with two rooms on each side. Two rooms were also provided on the upper floor and each of the four rooms had its own fireplace. In addition, spaces for smoking bacon could be made within the chimney and bread ovens inserted on the lower floor. The availability of bricks and the new style of construction led to what has been called the 'Great Rebuilding' of England and many of the picturesque timber-framed houses date from this time.

Another building that survives from this time is the former *White Lion Inn* on the Portsmouth Road. The trim 18th-century façade of this building actually hides a much older structure. In the 1930s a fireplace was discovered in one of the bedrooms which had the inscription '*Jhon Knyght 1584*'. The origins of the building may go back a further hundred years, as the White Lion was the badge of Edward IV.

A Probate Inventory

A rare glimpse into the furnishings and contents of a house at this time is provided by the probate inventory, made in 1587, of the estate of Richard Taylor, a farmer who probably lived at Leigh Hill. The following is an extract:

In the Hall
Imprimis in the Hall, a fowlding
    Standard Table, and a Forme:
two Lyttle Stooles: and a Chaire .... ijs.
Itm three Brasse pots .... xvjs.
Itm Fowre Kettells: and two
    ould Caldrons togethe .... xxijs.
Itm a possnett and two old
    Skelletts part of a loom .... viijd
Itm a Chafinge dishe .... vjd.
Itm a Laver; three Latten
    Candlesticks and a Skumer .... iiijs
Itm old peytinge in the Hall hanging .... xijd
Itm an Awndyron, a Grydyron, a pote
    hanger: one spytt: a toasting yron:
    and two dripping pans .... vjs.
In the Bed Chamber behinde
    the hall at the West end
Itm viij pewter platters: three pewter
    dishes: iiij pottingers: one Sawcer:
one old Bason: a quart and a pynt pott
    of pewter: Salt Seller: Six spoones .... xiiijs.
Itm a Cupborde with a Lock:
    and four old chests .... viijs.
Itm two boorded bedstedd
    with Testerns paynted .... iis.vid.
Itm for three paynted clothes there

The inventory goes on to list everything in the loft, the entry (porch), the buttery, the kitchen and barn, together with the crops standing in the field. The total value put upon the estate was a little over £20, which was a considerable sum in those days.

Almost at the closing of the century, on 6 December 1599, the will of John Abbot of Cobham was proved. An unusual item listed among the bequests is 'a swarm of bees at William Steedwell's house'. The following century was to see great changes not only to the landscape but also to the very fabric of the constitutional and political scene that were quick to be reflected at the local level.

Seven

THE SEVENTEENTH CENTURY

It is in the early years of the 17th century that local records begin to reveal something more of the lives of ordinary people in Cobham.

Law, Order and Care of the Poor

Care of the sick and elderly had been a responsibility of the parish since Elizabethan times, and in 1630 we find the first account of the distribution of Smith's Charity, a fund that is still paid to the parish and now forms part of Cobham Combined Charities. Henry Smith had been born in Wandsworth in or about 1545 and died in 1628. He was a salter by trade who grew rich and purchased estates in various parts of England. He had no children and during his lifetime created a number of charitable trusts for poor relief one of which was for the relief of the poor of over two hundred specific parishes of which Cobham was one. The Church-wardens' Book records the following:

Robert Best very aged . . . . .4s. 9d.
Thomas Mershe impotent . . . . 4s.
Robert Montague having 5 children . . .4s. 5d.
Charles Martyr in time of sickness . . . . 6s.
Widdow Goose for 5 children . . . . .5s. 6d.
Ellin Goose whose husband
    was prest for a souldier . . . . .4s. 11d.

Also in 1630 local property owners were taxed to pay for the churchyard palings, or fence,

and the Churchwardens' Book contains a complete list of ratepayers of the time. 'Mr Sutton' was responsible for the 'style gate' and 'Mr Downes', who was one of the largest property owners, was responsible for four 'paines'.

In August 1613 a Cobham innkeeper, Thomas Hemingway, landlord of the *Swan* at Street Cobham, found himself in trouble with the law. The King's Privy Council issued 'A warrant to Raymund Osbaston, one of the messengers of his Majestie's Chamber, to make his repayre to Cobham in the county of Surrey, and there to apprehend Thomas Hemingway, innehoulder, and to bring him forthwith before the lords.' On the same day there was also issued 'A warrant the Keeper of the Marshalsey to receive into his custody the person of Thomas Hemingway, and to keep him prisoner until further directions.' Neither Hemingway's misdemeanour or the outcome of the matter is recorded.

Sir Humphrey Lynde

Cobham's most famous resident at this time was the theologian Sir Humphrey Lynde, who in his will desired 'to be decently buried in Cobham Chancell above the step without pompe'. The entry of his burial in 1636 in the parish register notes that he was 'famous for his writing in defence of the Protestant Religion'. Lynde's funeral sermon, containing a detailed eulogy on his life and character, was preached by his friend Dr Featley, another well-known puritan of the time and a chaplain to the King.

Lynde's daughter Margaret had married Vincent Gavell, who became lord of the manor. When Vincent died Margaret married again, her second husband being the Reverend John Platt, rector of West Horsley, who was to feature strongly in the episode of the Diggers. Although Sir Humphrey Lynde's memorial did not survive the various 19th-century restorations of St Andrew's, one of the church's oldest monuments does date from this time. It is to the memory of Aminadab Cooper, 'Citizen and Merchant Taylor of London', who died in 1618. Close by is the memorial to Sarah Coxe, the daughter of Ralph Coxe, 'Silkman and Citizen of London', who died in 1631.

Schooling

In 1642 a charity school was founded in Cobham with an endowment in land. This may have been the school of John Goldwire, Gentleman, who in the same year contributed ten shillings to a collection 'for the speedie contribution and loan towards the reliefe of his majesties distressed subjects of the Kingdom of Ireland'. Mr Goldwire's 'scollars' contributed between them seven shillings and sixpence.

The World Turned Upside Down

The reign of Charles I saw unprecedented events that led to the outbreak of a bloody civil war in 1642 which divided families and communities. The King's execution resulted in the English Republic. People living at the time said it seemed as though the world had been 'turned upside down'. With one exception, no written accounts exists which record public feelings in Cobham. However, it is certain that the village was affected by the outbreak of the conflict between King and Parliament. In 1642, after an abortive attempt to take London, the King had retreated first to the Kingston area and then to Oatlands Palace at Weybridge. Shortly afterwards he withdrew to Oxford leaving this part of the country under Parliamentary control.

One of the minor incidents of the Civil War had begun at Surrey in October 1642 when George Wither, the poet, was appointed Governor of Farnham Castle. Soon after his appointment Wither and his men were forced to retreat from Farnham to Kingston, passing along the old Portsmouth Road through Cobham in order to avoid the Royalist cavalry at Bagshot and Prince Rupert, who was advancing to Weybridge.

Like other towns and villages in the Parliamentary controlled area Cobham was expected to contribute to the war effort, and in 1643 a warrant was issued to the High Constable of Elmbridge 'for the bringing in of horses, money etc'. Although Cobham was assessed for 'one horse or £4.10s.' at this time, parish accounts drawn up two years later state that 14 horses were made available in the service of Parliament and that 29 horses were said to have been seized during the war. In addition, Cobham's free quarter expenses for members of the Parliamentary army were among the highest recorded in Surrey and are unique in their reference to parishioners who were 'forced to forsake their habitation' as a result of these pressures.

A
DECLARATION
TO THE
Powers of England,
AND

To all the Powers of the VVorld, ſhewing the
Cauſe why the common People of England have begun, and gives conſent to dig up, manure, and ſow Corn upon *George*-Hill in *Surrey* ; by thoſe that have ſubſcribed, and
thouſands more that give conſent.

OR,

The ſtate of Community opened, and preſen-
ted to the Sons of Men.

BY

William Everard,	*Chriſtopher Clifford*,	*William Hoggrill*,
Iohn Palmer,	*Iohn Barker*,	*Robert Sawyer*,
Iohn South,	*Ferrard Winſtanley*,	*Thomas Eder*,
Iohn Courton,	*Richard Goodgroom*,	*Henry Bickerſtaffe*,
William Taylor,	*Thomas Starre*,	*Iohn Taylor*, &c.

Beginning to plant, and manure the waſt Land upon *George-Hill*,
neare *Walton*, in the County of *Surrey*.

LONDON,

Printed for *Giles Calvert*, at the Black Spread-Eagle at the
Weſt end of *Pauls*. **1649.**

46 *Gerrard Winstanley's* A Declaration To The
Powers of England.

In 1647 John Platt, now lord of the manor, granted a lease of Cobham Court to John Inwood of Walton-on-Thames. When the Civil War began Inwood had become a supporter of the Parliamentary Cause and in many documents he is described as Captain Inwood. In a certificate dated 6 May 1645 it was recorded that Inwood had 'adventured his life under Sir William Waller in Parliamentary service for which £100 was due to him'. During the period 1649-53 Inwood was one of a small group of men made responsible by Parliament for surveying Crown lands in Surrey preparatory to their sale.

With its long tradition of radical Protestantism, we can be fairly certain that feelings in Cobham would have run strong concerning the King and his Catholic wife. It was the vicar, William King, who gave voice to his feelings but, following an unexpected Parliamentary defeat in 1644, the parish registers record that he 'did about the beginning of Sep. leave this Parish, being afraid lest he should have been taken by some of the King's party and punished for speaking against his Majesty and justifying the proceedings of the Parliament whose Forces were about this time totally defeated in Cornwall. And having left his Vicarage he never returned to it again, but was in a short time prepar'd to the Rectory of Ashstead.' For the next 12 years Cobham was without a regular pastor and relied upon non-resident ministers such as John Goldwire, an ordained minister and schoolmaster who in 1645 helped compile the parish accounts.

One of the last armed engagements of the Civil War took place at nearby Kingston in 1648, when the Earl of Holland decided to raise an army in the town to rescue the King from imprisonment on the Isle of Wight. His main allies were the Duke of Buckingham and his young brother, Lord Francis Villiers. The whole enterprise was a fiasco and resulted in the death of Villiers and 20 officers and soldiers.

Gerrard Winstanley and the Diggers

Although the Civil War did not see any military action in Cobham, it did spark an important and well recorded episode that shook not only the local community but also give cause for concern at a national level. The war had resulted in the breakdown of political controls, censorship and church courts. Free discussion followed on many previously taboo subjects such as democracy, equality, land ownership and the abolition of the aristocracy and the state church. For many the Bible became the source of all wisdom and direction and many preachers and teachers emerged with their own individualistic interpretation of current events. One such man was Gerrard Winstanley, a native of Wigan who later moved down to London as a clothing apprentice.

After experiencing severe financial difficulties Winstanley left London for Surrey. His name first appears in the Cobham area in 1646 when he, with others, was accused of digging peat from the common without the licence of the lord of the manor. By 1649 Winstanley was herding cows for his neighbours in the vicinity of Cobham and Walton-on-Thames. It was perhaps as a result of this personal misfortune that he experienced intense soul-searching and believed that God spoke to him in a trance with the words 'Work together, eat bread together; declare this all abroad.' Winstanley felt called to break what he termed the 'Norman Yoke', the system imposed upon the country in 1066 which upheld the right of a few to own most of the land. Winstanley believed that the earth was created 'a common treasury for all'.

For many, Winstanley is now considered as the father of English socialism, and certainly his writings provide a blueprint for a utopian socialist state that was way ahead of its time. Others before Winstanley had committed to paper their ideas for the perfect state but none had been prepared to take his brave step and turn words into action. Winstanley wrote, 'Words and writing were all Nothing and must die, for action is the life of all and if thou dost not act, thou dost nothing.' In fulfilment of his divine commission Winstanley gathered about him a small group of followers who became known as the Diggers or True Levellers. The group set about clearing and planting common land on St George's Hill near Cobham. Their actions brought them into conflict with the local lord of the manor, Sir Francis Drake, who actually owned the land, as well as with some of the manorial tenants who had rights in the commons. The landowners sent a petition to the Council of State, who asked the Commander in Chief of the Army, General Thomas, Lord Fairfax, to investigate this 'great number of persons gathered together about Cobham in a tumultuous and riotous manner'.

There were exaggerated claims that the Diggers 'doe threaten to pull downe and levell all parke pales, and lay open, and intend to plant there very shortly. They give out they will bee four or five thousand within 10 dayes.' In fact, Winstanley maintained that the Diggers 'will neither meddle with Corn, Cattell, nor inclosed land, but only in the Commons'. Fairfax's representative, Captain Gladman, came to Cobham ready for a fight, but on arrival his assessment of the situation was that 'the business was not worth the writing or taking notice of'. However, it was arranged for Winstanley and a fellow digger, William Everard, to appear before Fairfax the next day. Famously, both Diggers refused to remove their hats in the presence of the General who they considered was 'but their

47 *General Sir Thomas Fairfax, Commander in Chief of Cromwell's army.*

fellow creature'. They explained their plans and convinced Fairfax that they meant no harm. Any rights in the commons claimed by the lords of the manors had, as Winstanley explained, been 'cut off with the King's head'. The General was initially sympathetic and let them go with a warning.

Fairfax later visited the Digger colony when passing through Cobham on the Portsmouth Road. He was moderately impressed by what he saw. Despite the fact that there had been a number of skirmishes with local people, he considered the Diggers constituted no real threat to the central government, and thought that they could be left to the mercy of the local justices.

In Cobham, the Diggers' principal antagonist was the lord of the manor, John Platt. An action for trespass was brought against the Diggers in the court at Kingston upon Thames. The Diggers asked to be allowed to defend themselves, being unwilling on principle and financially unable to retain their own lawyer, but this plea was dismissed and a hostile jury found against them. Unable to pay the fines and costs of the action, the Diggers saw their goods and cattle carried off by the court bailiffs. Platt continued to stir up opposition, aided by other local landowners and manorial tenants. At a meeting held in the *White Lion* inn at Cobham, when 'a great deal of sack and tobacco was consumed', local traders were persuaded to refuse to serve the Diggers.

The Diggers eventually left St George's Hill and moved to the Little Heath at Cobham where they remained for about a year. However, it was here in 1650 that the 11 acres of corn planted by the Diggers and half a dozen temporary houses were destroyed in a bloody action led by Platt and Thomas Sutton, the impropriator of the living. Shortly before this event two emissaries had been sent out by the Cobham Diggers to similar colonies now established in other parts of the Home Counties and beyond. With them went a letter signed by Winstanley and 21 others asking for financial support, but it was too late. After the events at the Little Heath the community appears to have come to an end. Winstanley and 14 others were indicted for disorderly and unlawful assembly.

Many of the Diggers' names are known from Winstanley's tracts and petitions but little is known of their fate. In 1650 Winstanley and some of his 'poor bretheren' hired themselves to Lady Eleanor Davies of Pirton, Hertfordshire, an eccentric lady who believed she had the gift of prophecy. Much of Winstanley's life after this is shrouded in mystery, although he does appear to have come back to Cobham for a while before returning to London. Winstanley's first wife Susan was the daughter of William King, a London surgeon who owned property in Cobham. King made over this property to the use of his daughter and her husband and made provision in his will that it was to pass to Winstanley's heirs if he and Susan should have no children. Susan's early death meant that Winstanley became once more a man of property and he is listed among the tenants of Ham in Cobham in 1662. His name is also found in the Cobham parish records as both a churchwarden and an overseer of the poor. The registers record the baptisms of three of the children born to his second wife between 1665 and 1669, and in 1671 and 1672 Winstanley is recorded as one of the two Chief Constables of the Elmbridge Hundred.

This apparent prosperity and rejection by Winstanley of his earlier radical views may have triggered the criticism levelled by the radical preacher Lawrence Clarkson in 1660, who wrote of a 'most shameful retreat from George's Hill, with a spirit of pretended universality, to become a real Tithe-gather of proprietary'. A man named Gerrard Winstanley, who died a Quaker in London in 1676, is likely to have been a Cobham Digger, especially as Winstanley had links with the Quakers in Kingston upon Thames in 1647. Winstanley's writings seem to reflect the Quaker influence and it was even suggested by Thomas Comber in 1678 that it was

48 *Mole Cottage, Church Street. This 17th-century house was home to the King family, who may have been related by marriage to Gerrard Winstanley.*

Winstanley and not George Fox who was 'the Institutor' of Quakerism.

The Diggers were virtually forgotten for two centuries but academics, politicians and activists have recently brought Winstanley into the limelight and a great many books and articles have been published about both the man and his message. The events at St George's Hill and Cobham have been featured on television and radio as well as in a full-length film and were probably the most important to take place in the history of Cobham; Winstanley must rank as Cobham's most important resident.

Three hundred and fifty years after this episode, Cobham has a memorial to Winstanley and the Diggers as part of trail around the Borough of Elmbridge. Winstanley is already commemorated on a monument erected in Moscow just after the Russian Revolution, whose leaders seem to have been influenced by Winstanley's writings.

Cobham's Quakers
Although Thomas Comber had called Gerrard Winstanley the 'Institutor' of

Quakerism, there is no evidence to suggest that it was he who started this movement in the 17th century. However, and not surprisingly, Cobham did become a Quaker centre by the 1670s and at least one known Cobham Digger, John Hayman, seems to have become a Quaker. In 1665 John Downes, a wheeler, George Scrub, a collar maker, and William Lock, a butcher, all of Cobham gave evidence to the magistrates that Ephraim Carter, a butcher living at Norwood Farm, and Thomas Barton, a baker, both of whom were Quakers, had held illegal meetings in Carter's house. Both Carter and Barton were fined and committed to the White Lion prison in Southwark. Imprisonment did not discourage Carter and his name continues to appear over the following years in Kingston Quaker records. In 1673 Carter allowed his home to be used for the Quarterly Meeting and he later played a prominent role in the building of a local Meeting House. Also in 1673 it was reported that the Cobham Meeting was attended by 'many of the world's people' and it had clearly become the centre of a wide area of Surrey Quaker activity. In 1682 Ephraim Carter was appointed by the Cobham Vestry as surveyor of the highways for Street Cobham.

In 1676 Cobham's Quakers purchased a piece of land and four years later a Meeting House was opened. However, the number of Quakers appears to have declined in the following century and by 1725 there was one Quaker family living in Cobham. The last Quarterly Meeting held in Cobham was in 1735 and in 1739 the building was sold to Samuel Hetherington for £15. The burial ground was excluded from the sale and not disposed of until the 1840s. The remaining Cobham Friends had probably long since transferred to the meeting at nearby Esher. The site of the Cobham Meeting House and its burial ground is uncertain. However, a deed of 1849 refers to a 'Quaker's Close' in the area of World's End at the rear of the site until recently occupied by the Central Garage on the old Portsmouth Road.

Monarchy Restored

The restoration of Charles II in 1660 prompted Parliament to ask the nation to make a 'free and voluntary present' to the King. Though voluntary, it is evident that many persons thought it prudent to contribute. A full list of Cobham donors has survived and it is interesting to note that even men like John Inwood, who had fought for Parliament, considered it politic to contribute twenty shillings. John Inwood's uncle, Sir William Inwood, was also living in Cobham at this time and contributed fifty shillings, the second highest amount in the parish. Sir William had not been active in Surrey during the Civil War and this suggests he may have been a Royalist sympathiser.

The largest donor in Cobham was William Carpenter who contributed the substantial sum of £5. Three years after making this generous gift Carpenter was granted a coat-of-arms in 1663 as a reward for his services as 'King's Messenger'. Carpenter was related to Samuel Carpenter who served as Treasurer of Pennsylvania from 1685 to 1711 and was named by William Penn in his will as the trustee of his property in America. Another of those rewarded by the King was the wife of Francis Wyndham, who was granted a fishery at Cobham Bridge. Anne Wyndham and her husband had sheltered Charles in

49 *The* Royal Oak *from a postcard of c.1905.*

1651 in their home in the Somerset village of Trent after his disastrous defeat at the Battle of Worcester.

Both the restoration of the monarchy and the battle of Worcester were commemorated in the naming of *The Royal Oak*, a pub that formerly stood on the junction of Anyards Road and the Portsmouth Road. Charles II narrowly escaped capture by hiding in an oak tree after this battle. *The Royal Oak* was pulled down in 1974 and replaced by Coveham. Stern puritanical laws had been imposed during the period of the Commonwealth and in 1653 Lawrence Johnson of Cobham had been presented at the Assize for keeping a disorderly alehouse. The restoration of the monarchy resulted in their relaxation or abolition. In 1662 William Kidwell, landlord of the *White Lion* at Cobham, was granted permission by the local justices 'to keep a common victualling house for the space of one whole year … in the house where he now dwelleth at Cobham' if he 'shall not … admit or suffer any unlawful games to be used in his house or any evil rule or disorder to be kept there'. Included among 'unlawful games' were dice, cards, tables, shovel groat, ninepins and a game called Ockay.

In 1673 John Aubrey wrote, 'At Cobham is a medicated Spring of the nature of Epsham which was discovered about three years since by a country-man using it in his food: as also giving to his pigges which he putt to fatting: I am told at the bottome of this Well are Stones like Bristow-diamonds', crystals of colourless quartz worn by ladies of rank. Other spas could be found at Spa Bottom between Cobham and Esher and at Jessop's Well at Oxshott. If they had been fully exploited these wells might could have made Cobham into a spa town like nearby Epsom.

50   *The* White Lion *from a postcard of c.1920.*

51   *The spa and well house at Goose Green, Downside c.1930.*

Samuel Pepys at Cobham

In addition to licensing the local alehouses, the Justices also dealt with matters relating to maintenance of roads and bridges. Maintenance was the responsibility of the local people and failure to undertake the necessary work resulted in the matter being taken to the Surrey Quarter Sessions. In 1662 the inhabitants of Cobham were ordered to repair the 'Fayre Mile'. The Portsmouth Road was an uncomfortable and sometimes hostile road to travel. In 1677 the Clerk of the Survey at Portsmouth wrote to the Secretary of State to say that on 'Monday this week our coaches were both robbed coming from London by four horsemen, a mile or two this side of Cobham'. In 1688 Samuel Pepys recorded in his diary how he and his wife travelled 'to Gilford, losing our way for three or four miles about Cobham'. In 1661 it was reported that 'Downe Bridge' was in need of repair, and in 1671 Commissioner J. Tippetts wrote to the Navy Commissioners stating that he 'arrived late on Friday, the ways being bad, and Cobham Bridge part carried away with the flood, and the river too deep to be passed through'.

Trades and Occupations

Following the upheaval cause by the Civil War, there was a shortage of small change during the period 1650 to 1670 which led local tradesmen in some parts of the country to issue their own official small coins, known as trade tokens. Two such tokens are known to have been issued in Cobham by Francis Tyrill in 1667 and by Thomas King at around the same time. Thomas King may have lived at Mole Cottage, Church Street. The core of this house dates from the early 17th century and inscribed on the timbers and plasterwork inside the property are the date 1645 and the initials WK, which may stand for William King. Close by is Church Stile House, which was rebuilt in the 1620s by Edward Fawcett, a London tallow chandler who had taken a lease on the property in 1614.

Other 17th-century properties still to be seen in Cobham are World's End Cottage at Street Cobham and Woronoake, close to the *Running Mare* in Tilt Road. The latter seems to have been built as a one-room cottage and was probably once the home of a cottager who got leave of the lord of the manor to

52 *Seventeenth-century trade tokens of Thomas King and Francis Tyrill of Cobham.*

enclose a small piece of the land on the edge of the Tilt Common which then stretched from here to Ashford Farm House. The builder chose the site wisely since it is just above the flood plain of the river Mole.

In 1662 a practice of taxing householders on the number of hearths in their home was started. This usually amounted to two shillings per hearth, but the hearth tax, as it became known, was very unpopular and only lasted until 1689. The only surviving hearth tax list for the parish of Cobham is that of 1664 and it helps to indicate who the wealthiest property owners were at this time. Robert Gavell of Cobham Court, with 13 taxable hearths, topped the list, followed by John Downes of Downe Place and Richard Carter, the minister, each with 11 hearths. Sir William Inwood, the impropriator, was taxed for eight hearths. Also high on the list with nine hearths was William Carpenter, who had made such a generous donation to the King's restoration. Carpenter died in 1672 and was buried in Cobham church. A note in the church books states that it was at his expense that 'the church was ceiled'. A detailed probate inventory of the contents of his house

53 *Old Cottage, The Ridings, from a photograph of c.1890.*

confirms he was a man of considerable wealth living in a house with five chambers, or bedrooms, as well as a 'Great Parlour', 'Little Parlour', hall, kitchen and dairy. Although no indication is given of where this house stood, the hearth tax lists Carpenter under Downside, and a document of 1749, with the Cobham Park estate deeds, refers to William Carpenter as having lived at a property called 'Bridgelands' which Robert Gavell had sold to Viscountess Lanesborough in 1708. The present Cobham Park now occupies the site of 'Bridgelands'.

Whilst most local occupations at this time were linked to the land and to farming, Cobham still had two mills. That at Cobham was used for grinding corn but the mill at Downside appears to have been used for paper making as early as 1687. In 1691 the probate inventory of John Bicknell of Cobham includes all the raw materials and equipment for making paper, which seems to indicate that he was working at Downside. In 1652 Francis Sutton of Cobham is recorded as a tanner. He was probably working at or near Cedar House, where there was a plentiful supply of water and water power.

Skins of another sort were the concern of local warreners. The Normans had introduced rabbits into this country and by the 17th century their keeping had become very popular among landowners. The rabbits, or conies, provided a valuable source of meat and fur and were kept in large warrens that were enclosed either by long perimeter banks of earth or by stone walls. The sandy nature of the soil in the Cobham area provided excellent sites for warrens and sites are known to have existed at Painshill, Cobham Court and Oxshott. In 1633 Thomas Sutton of Cobham had leased the estate of Heywood to Richard Phillips of Cobham together with 'all that stocke and warren of conyes and conny burrowes with appurtenances as the same as are now planted upon parcel of the premises'.

In 1618 the well-known cartographer Nicholas Lane drew the earliest known map of any part of Cobham, an estate called Oxdownes, later called Stokesheath. John of Milbourne had granted this estate to William Brockhole in 1374. The property remained in the Brockhole family until 1579, when it was granted to George Evelyn. Included in the estate was a warren and warrener's cottage that still stands in The Ridings, off Sandy Lane. This house, which dates from the late 16th century, is now called Old Cottage. In 1649 the warren was leased by George Evelyn of Wotton to William Phillips of Cobham and the property was described as being 'late in the tenure of Anthony Wren', probably the same Anthony Wren who joined Gerrard Winstanley and the Diggers at this time. The 1664 Hearth Tax records a house with two hearths here.

In 1664 Richard Crowcher or Crutcher of Walton on Thames, warrener and husbandman, stole a coney hutch trap from William Carpenter who, as we have seen, was one of the wealthiest people living in Cobham at this time. The Quarter Sessions records for this action refer to Carpenter as 'one of

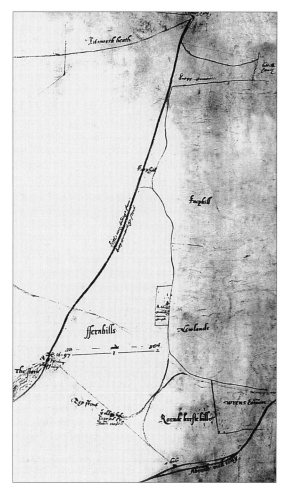

54 *Extract from Nicholas Lane's 1618 map of Oxdownes. The small rectangular plot between Fernhills and Newlands is marked 'A Cottage called the Warren House'.*

the gentlemen of his majestys privye chamber extraordinary'. One of the more common occupations at this time was that of blacksmith. In the late 17th century Robert Burgess, a blacksmith, lived in a house on the road to Downside opposite the entrance to Cobham Park. However, Burgess was evidently more than just a blacksmith and in 1682 he signed an agreement with the churchwardens of St George's, Esher to maintain their clock. It is likely that this clock,

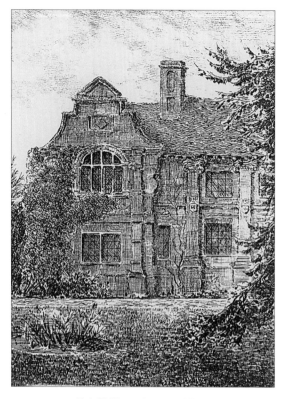

55   *Slyfield House from an old engraving.*

which is still in working order, was actually constructed by Burgess.

Another Revolution

The closing years of the 17th century saw the so called 'Glorious Revolution' which brought to the throne of England the Dutch Prince William of Orange. To secure the new King's position, in 1696 his subjects were required to put their names to a declaration of loyalty, known as the Association Oath. The names of 106 Cobham men are found on the Elmbridge list headed by Robert Gavell, William Weston, and Lionel Coles the minister.

Not everyone in England was in favour of William being offered the throne and, according to some accounts, it was at nearby Slyfield House at Stoke D'Abernon that the arrest took place of Sir John Fenwick, soldier, conspirator and Jacobite sympathiser. Fenwick had concocted a plot to shoot William III as he was on his way to hunt in Richmond Park, but the plan was discovered. According to the Surrey historian William Bray, Sir John 'was taken at a house by the side of the road from Great Bookham to Stoke D'Abernon', which suggests Slyfield House. Local legend has it that Fenwick was arrested in the Cedar Bedroom at 5 a.m. one June day in 1696; history records that he was executed on Tower Hill on 28 January of the following year. It is curious to note that Sir John did have an indirect role to play to in the death of the King. The King had confiscated Fenwick's horse and it stumbled over the molehill in Bushey Park, which resulted in the King developing pneumonia and dying.

The final record of Cobham's 17th-century residents is found in the 1699 churchwardens' account of the sums 'Collected on His Majesties Brief for the Vandors & French Refugees'. The Vandors or Waldenses were a protestant religious community to which the English government paid an annual subsidy. Robert Gavell and William Weston contributed one pound each. The next two largest gifts were from Dr Barton and Robert Porter, who each gave five shillings. Robert Burgess, the blacksmith, gave sixpence.

Eight

THE AGE OF IMPROVEMENT

In many ways the English countryside in 1700 had changed little since the Middle Ages but by the end of the 18th century Britain was fast developing into a prosperous industrial nation with a vast empire around the globe.

Enclosure of Open Fields and Commons
The national trend was reflected in Cobham, where the most dramatic change was the enclosure of the old open fields and commons, or waste, that had for so long been a feature of both the appearance and life of the village. A certain amount of enclosure had taken place in Cobham before the 18th century but this had usually been done by mutual agreement between the parties involved. By the 18th century it was the practice to petition for an Act of Parliament, and leading landowners usually did this as it was they who would benefit most. Between 1750 and 1800 the landscape was transformed and the English countryside became that we know today, one of fields, hedges and scattered farms.

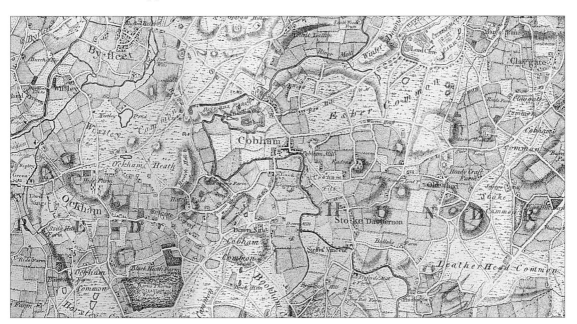

56 *Extract from John Rocque's map of Surrey showing Cobham and the surrounding area in the middle of the 18th century.*

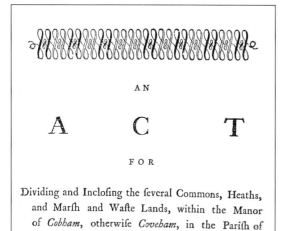

An

A C T

FOR

Dividing and Inclofing the feveral Commons, Heaths, and Marfh and Wafte Lands, within the Manor of *Cobham*, otherwife *Coveham*, in the Parifh of *Cobham*, in the County of *Surrey*.

Cobham, Surrey.

P A R T I C U L A R S,

AND

CONDITIONS OF SALE,

OF FOUR PIECES OF

VALUABLE UNINCLOSED FREEHOLD LAND,

Part of *COBHAM TILT*, called *The* HOOK,

Adjoining the RIVER *MOLE*;

Being Part of the "Commons, Heaths, and Marfh and Wafte Lands,"

In the Parifh of *COBHAM*, within the County of *SURREY*,

Directed to be divided and inclofed by virtue of an Act of Parliament paffed in the Year 1793, which are allotted and fet out by the Commiffioners appointed by the faid Act, agreeable to the Powers contained therein, towards defraying the Charges and Expences of paffing and carrying the faid Act into execution:

Which will be SOLD by AUCTION,

By Mr. *Y O U N G*,

At the WHITE LION INN, at *COBHAM STREET*,

On MONDAY the 2d Day of *DECEMBER*, 1793, at Twelve o'Clock,

IN FOUR LOTS.

57 *The enclosure of Cobham's Open Fields and Commons took place by Acts of Parliament in 1779 and 1793.*

58 *Some of the land enclosed on the Tilt was sold by auction in 1793 to defray the expenses of the enclosure procedure. (Surrey History Service)*

Sadly, for some the social effects of enclosure were disastrous. Small farmers and cottagers were driven off the soil as the land was enclosed. A contemporary rhyme summed up their predicament:

The Law doth punish man or woman
Who steals the goose from off the common
But set the greater felon loose
Who steals the common from the goose.

However, enclosure was economically necessary to bring the land into profitable production and was taking place all over the country.

First came the enclosure of the old open fields of the parish into neat, rectangular hedged and manageable units. It was Cobham's lord of the manor, Thomas Page of Pointers, who, in 1779, together with William Abington of Leigh Hill House, John Balchin of Cedar House, Benjamin Bond Hopkins of Painshill, Andrew Ramsay of Hatchford Park and others obtained a private

Act of Parliament for 'dividing and inclosing the common and open fields within the parish'. This was one of the earliest enclosure acts in Surrey and dealt with the cultivated strips that had dwindled in extent from 482 acres in 1598 to 370 acres at the time of the Act. The Act for enclosing the common fields ordered 'that the present road leading from Street Cobham to Church Cobham (Between Streets) be made forty feet wide' and that 'the bridle road leading from Church Cobham to the Royal Oak alehouse running between Churchfield and the Anyards shall be continued five feet wide and kept in repair at the expense of Sutton Porter'. Sutton Porter was the landlord of the *Royal Oak* which stood on the site now occupied by Coveham, and the bridle road still exists as an unmade road at the rear of the houses on the west side of Anyards Road.

At this time there were two gates across Between Streets: one was at the junction with the Portsmouth Road and the other near to the present High Street. In 1786 it was decided to remove these gates since they were causing a nuisance and there had been 'several accidents having happened by their obstructing the Road'. The chief complainant was Alexander Raby and it is likely that the gates were proving a great nuisance to the increasingly heavy traffic passing through to his ironworks at Downside Mill.

Enclosure of the common fields was followed in 1793 by the more dramatic enclosure of the commons on which many of the poorest tenants depended for their grazing rights. According to the preamble to the Act there were several large open commons, heaths and marshes and wastelands in Cobham, and across these were to be laid new roads not less than forty feet wide and no trees were to be planted on either side nearer to each other than fifty feet. Certain areas were to be set aside for gravel pits for the construction and maintenance of the new roads. Some of the roads constructed can be seen nowadays in the long straight stretches of the Portsmouth Road, Fairmile Lane, Stoke Road, Bookham Common Road and Horsley Road. The total amount enclosed was over 1,000 acres. Heather gave place to crops on much of the Fairmile, and the grass of Downside Common, hitherto 'consumed by herds of little horses', gave way to excellent yields of corn.

Those copyhold tenants of the manor and freeholders with rights in the commons whose properties were valued at £10 or more were invited to submit claims to the commissioners for allocation of a piece of land in lieu of their extinguished rights. For those with properties valued at under £10,

three hundred acres of common land was left unenclosed for grazing and for cutting turf and heath for fuel. The largest common was the Tilt, which stretched from Leigh Hill through to the parish boundary with Stoke D'Abernon. The land was carved up and allocated to qualifying copyholders. The chief beneficiaries were those with reasonable existing land holdings who were then able to exchange with other landowners and merge their holdings to create compact farms and estates such as Cobham Park, Cobham Court, Eaton Farm and Leigh Hill Farm.

Pioneers in Agriculture

Enclosure resulted in a far more economic and manageable system of farming and was assisted by the great changes that were being

59 *John Southey, 15th Lord Somerville from a contemporary engraving.*

60 *Fairmile Farm from the 1829 watercolour by E. Hassell. (British Library)*

introduced into agriculture. Two pioneer agriculturists had estates in Cobham: Lord Somerville and Thomas Ruggles both farmed on the Fairmile.

John Southey, 15th Lord Somerville, who acquired Fairmile Farm in the early years of the 19th century, had invented a number of farm implements. The *Dictionary of National Biography* says he 'held advanced views on a variety of subjects ranging from agricultural education, experimental farms, the slaughtering of animals, old age pensions and other rural subjects.' Somerville was also the second largest owner of merino sheep in England and did much to improve sheep breeding. The largest owner of merinos was George III, or 'Farmer George' as he was popularly known, and he and Somerville took a close interest in each other's activities. In 1810 Somerville's merino flock was sold by auction at Fairmile Farm and fetched £10,000. Somerville was also a keen sportsman, both in the hunting field and as an angler, and a close friend of Sir Walter Scott, who was a neighbour to Somerville's estates in Scotland.

William Duckett, who invented the drill plough, lived in nearby Esher, but land tax records reveal he was farming land on Cobham Fairmile in the late 1780s. George III used to visit Duckett on his farm and took a great interest in his experiments.

In the middle years of the 18th century Thomas Ruggles inherited through his mother's family, the Brices, a large old Cobham property which stood overlooking the River Mole. Known as Brickhouse it had probably acquired that name because it was one of the first brick houses to be erected in the village. It later became known as Leigh Hill House and then Leigh Place and was demolished in the 1930s. Ruggles also owned Knipp Hill Farm, which adjoined Fairmile Farm, and he corresponded at length with his friend Arthur Young concerning his pioneering ideas on farmland management and arboriculture which he practised at Cobham. Young, who was secretary to the Board of Agriculture in 1793, wrote a number of books and is best known for his 'Annals of Agriculture', to which Ruggles was a regular contributor. His contributions are particularly important as he was one of the first to discuss the planting of what became known as the 'ferme ornée', or picturesque farm. He also wrote an important article on the 'The Planting And The Use Of Trees', in which he writes of his 'enquiries … made in the County of Surry, my own observations there, where I have planted some thousands of the different sorts (pines and firs) but particularly scotch pine and larch'. Ruggles grew these trees in plantations on the Fairmile, and the Scots Pine, which he and others introduced, has now become a familiar feature of the heathlands of Surrey.

61 Leigh Place (formerly Leigh Hill House) once the home of Thomas Ruggles, from a postcard of c.1910.

Ruggles' care also extended to those employed on the land, and in 1797 he wrote *The History of the Poor, their Rights, Duties, and the law respecting them.* He eventually left Cobham for Spain's Hall, an imposing Tudor mansion on the outskirts of Finchingfield, Essex which he inherited from an uncle. Thomas Ruggles' neighbour on the Fairmile was James Cooper, who owned Eaton Farm and part of Fairmile Lane known at this time as 'Cooper's Lane'. In 1725 Cooper brought an action for the arrest of George Millett of Ewell, a barber who 'with three gentlemen and one servant whose names are not known went hunting in time of divine service into the standing corn' at Eaton Farm. This act of poaching was considered to be a 'dishonour to the Laws of God as well as being in contempt of His Majesties commands and in defiance of all the Statutes in that case'.

62 The Rev. Dr John Trusler from a wax portrait believed to have been made in 1786.

63   *St Andrew's church in 1822 from the watercolour by J. Hassell. This view from the north shows the exterior staircases that were constructed to give access to the galleries put up inside the church in the 18th century. (British Library)*

A local observer and commentator on the enclosures and farming locally was the Reverend Dr John Trusler, who made his home in Cobham in the 1780s. An eccentric divine and writer, Trusler lived for a short time in Ham Manor but later moved to Downside. He was the son of the proprietor of the public tea gardens in Marylebone and became a priest in 1759. He pursued a number of innovative ways to earn money, one of which was the printing in imitation handwriting of a collection of sermons which he sold for one shilling each in order to save clergy both study and the trouble of transcription. The bishops frowned upon this publication and discouraged its use. More successful was Trusler's *Practical Husbandry, or the Art of Farming with certainty of gain*, first published in 1780. It refers not only to local farming methods but also the special method of 'dead hedging' that was in use in Cobham at the time.

Local Administration – the Vestry and the Poor

Throughout the Middle Ages and into the Tudor period, local administration had been largely the responsibility of the manor courts. However, by the 18th century much of this had passed to the Vestry or parish meeting, which effectively became the parish council. The Vestry met regularly throughout the year, usually in the comfort of a tavern parlour, and several Cobham inns were used for this purpose until a permanent Vestry room was built adjoining the parish church.

Appointments by the Vestry included the churchwardens, whose office had by this time attracted many secular duties, the surveyor of the highways, and the petty constable, who was usually assisted by two headboroughs. All these were unpaid post and only held for a limited term of office. It was also the Vestry's function to appoint the parish beadle. Church attendance in the 18th century was considered desirable but not just for spiritual reasons. It was the place to see and be seen. The local aristocracy, gentry and farmers would attend and those in their employment were wise to put in an appearance. The medieval parish church of St Andrew was not large enough to take the growing congregation and it was decided that galleries should be constructed inside the building. Access to these was by way of wooden staircases inserted through the windows without any real concern for the ancient fabric or aesthetic appearance.

Minutes of a Vestry meeting held on 30 June 1799 record:

> At a meeting of the Committee appointed to regulate the Pews in the Church, it is ordered that in future all Gentlemen's Livery Servants shall sit in the Gallery on the south side of the Organ, that all women servants be placed in a pew on the left side next the Gallery and the two opposite ones, and also that all women strangers be placed there, and in the next adjoining Pew on the left hand, that all Farmer's servants, apprentices, journeymen and boys and girls sit in the right hand Chancel, the people in the workhouse in the left hand Chancel; that Wm. Watkins be appointed Beadle to attend the inhabitants to their Pews, and that he be provided with a coat and hat, and that each Pew have a Lock fixed as soon as convenient.

Another important function of the Vestry was the appointment of the overseers, whose job it was to collect the poor rate and organise and distribute relief to the needy.

The pace of change in the 18th century was not good for everyone. The rising population, enclosure of the commons, high prices during the war with France and the widespread unemployment that followed combined to create hardship and poverty and an increase in those needing parish assistance. A Poor Law had been introduced in the reign of Elizabeth I but the workhouse system was not made general by statute until 1723, out-relief being obtainable for those born in the parish. The maintenance of the poor was a heavy burden on parishioners and vagrants and paupers from other parishes were sent back to their place of settlement. In 1662 Elizabeth Pope 'a vagrant within the parish of Cobham', was ordered to be 'conveyed and carried by the constable of Cobham' to the parish of Great Bookham, which was her place of birth. In 1771 it was decided 'all persons that inhabit and work in our Parish not being Parishioners, without security shall be immediately ordered to bring certificates or be removed'.

Illegitimate children were also a burden on the poor rate as an illegitimate child took its settlement not from its parents but from its place of birth. In 1786 the Cobham Vestry agreed that 'the Officers do as soon as convenient execute the Warrant that they have got upon Dr Trusler for a Bastard sworn to him by his Maid'. This was the Reverend Dr John Trusler, the writer of agricultural and other books. Payment both in kind and money was made to the deserving poor and in 1775 'Richard Collingham's girl at Mr Woods' was given 'a pr. of shoes, 2 shifts, a pr. of stockings, an apron and under petticoat and gown, 2 aprons and hankerchive, a pr. of stays & a pr. of pattens'.

Prior to 1834 relief could be provided either by working on the parish roads or digging ditches, or in a workhouse or house of correction. The first mention of a workhouse in Cobham is in the parish registers in 1760. In 1772 the parish resolved that 'Tilthatch House be put in repair, and that Henry Goddard do go to the Workhouse, that is one of the apartments of the Workhouse'. The Tilt Hatch was a gate on the edge of the Tilt Common close to the 'The Old Fire Station'. In 1773 it was decided that Tilthatch House should be pulled down and rebuilt into three tenements. In 1780 the chambers in the workhouse were ceiled and the house whitewashed and in 1793 the room called the 'Shop' at the workhouse was repaired and the windows mended. In 1796 the master of the workhouse was ordered to send the poor to church every Sunday if the weather permitted and the following year the children were to be taught to read. In 1797 the Vestry 'ordered that a Badge containing the C.P. (Cobham Parish) in scarlet cloth be affixed to the clothes of every pauper in the workhouse' in accordance with an Act of 1697 that stated that everyone maintained by the parish should wear a badge of red or blue cloth with the initial of the parish. This badge of poverty was naturally resented, especially by the women, but those who refused to wear it were liable to have their allowance withdrawn, or could be committed to the House of Correction, there to be whipped and kept at hard labour for not more than twenty days.

The New Poor Law Act of 1832 led to the upheaval by which the poor were uprooted from their native parishes and made to live in bare barrack-like buildings far from their friends. In 1836 the Cobham Vestry resolved 'that it is of the opinion of this Vestry to be most advantageous for the parish to be united under the New Poor Law with the Epsom Union'. All able-bodied men and boys above the age of 13 were made to go the old Epsom Workhouse. Girls under 16, boys under 13 and mothers of children under seven went to Carshalton, and Leatherhead took aged and infirm men and Ewell aged and infirm women. Able-bodied women were divided between Carshalton, Leatherhead and Ewell. The building that served at the parish workhouse for many years still stands on the Upper Tilt as part of the row known as Korea Cottages. In addition there were a number of single-storey one-room cottages on either side of the main building and a similar row of cottages at the Lower Tilt next to 'The Old Fire Station'. These cottages were pulled down towards the end of the 19th century.

Cobham also had a 'Pest House', where those with infectious diseases were sent. This stood in an isolated spot off the road near Hatchford, opposite Pointers Farm and is first heard of in 1711. In 1783 the pest house was let to William Atkins who was to be paid ten shillings per week 'if there be any person with the Smallpox carried to the said house'. In 1792 the Vestry decided that the master of the workhouse 'should take the poor and every other casualty that may happen to the poor including small pox, broken bones and midwifery'. He was also to pay the doctor's salary. Smallpox was a common ailment at the end of the 18th century and in 1798 the Vestry decided that 'Whereas the Small Pox is now very prevalent in the Parish and to

64 *Cobham Tilt c.1870. The single-storey buildings are the old parish cottages. In 1896 the Cobham Parish Magazine reported that most of them were 'quite unfit for habitation'. They were eventually demolished and replaced by Gable Cottages in 1901.*

prevent an increase of expense it is thought expedient to inoculate all the Poor persons in the parish who shall be willing.' Dr Brown of Esher agreed to carry out this mass inoculation for the sum of 25 guineas.

The parish would often 'farm out' the poor to anyone who had enough accommodation and would take them for a fixed per capita payment. In 1786 it was agreed 'That if Port will take King's child from the Workhouse he shall be allowed one shilling pr. week.' Young men would often be apprenticed out from the workhouse and in 1775 it was agreed 'That Mr Raby [of Downside Mill] do take Benjamin son of Richard Bullen deceased, to put him Apprentice for seven years to one of his men.'

Maintenance of the highways was another responsibility of the Vestry and surveyors or 'waywardens' were appointed for Church Cobham, Street Cobham and Downside. Each man in the parish had to perform a fixed number of days labour in repairing the roads. In 1799 it was agreed 'That whereas Mr Davis has made application for a Road to be made to his house from Mr Freeland's farm to Norwood Farm, and whereas Mr Davis was now in arrears six days Duty, it was agreed that he shall be excused the 6 days duty in consequence of his making the said road.' Defence of the realm was the Vestry's concern, too, and the parish agreed to bear the 'expense of Arming and Clothing' those who volunteered their services in the event of an invasion by the French.

65　*Post Boys Row, Between Streets.*

The provision of schooling for ordinary people at this time was still very much a charitable affair largely in the hands of the philanthropic gentry. In the 1720s James Fox, lord of the manor, endowed a charity school for 40 children in Cobham. An increasing population and the need for improved mobility led to the establishment of turnpike roads throughout the country in the 18th century. Portsmouth had become the country's leading naval base and the road that linked it to London was turnpiked in stages. Cobham was on the stretch between Kingston and Petersfield which was turnpiked by an Act of Parliament in 1749. The Cobham Toll House stood close to the *Little White Lion*.

Roads, Bridges and Transport

Improvement in the roads led to improvement in methods of travel. Much of the traffic passing through Cobham at this time comprised commercial stage-coaches. Cobham's Fairmile was a favourite spot for drivers since they could, for the first time out of Kingston, get up some speed on this straight and firm stretch of the road. The *Universal Directory* of 1793 stated that:

> The Portsmouth mails pass through Cobham about 11 in the evening: and return at 4 in the morning. Two coaches from Cobham for London daily (except Sundays) set out at 7, and return at 6: fare inside 4s. outside 2s …. Coaches pass through this town for Chichester, Portsmouth, Arundel and Guildford. Waggons

also pass through for Guildford, Chichester and Portsmouth.

Local innkeepers hired out either chaises or horses on a mileage basis. They also employed post boys to return the vehicles or the horses to their inn who were often a good deal older than their title suggests. In the 1780s a row of terraced houses was built close the *White Lion* which is now called *Post Boys Row* and was home to several of the locally employed post boys. In the 1820s the *White Lion* was described as 'one of the best posting inns in the country'. The first mail coach was introduced in 1784 and Cobham's first post office was near the former *White Lion* inn. Local mail was delivered by paid letter carriers.

66 *Receipted bill from the* White Lion *inn, 1822.*

67 *The* Tartar Inn, *formerly* The Ship. *From an early 20th-century postcard.*

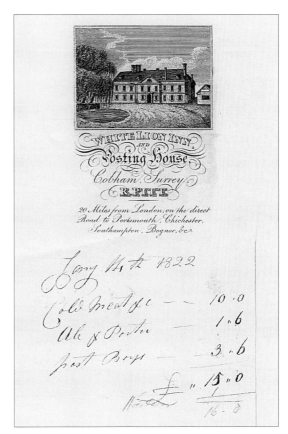

68   *The Red Rover coach passing through Cobham, from a 19th-century engraving.*

69   *Cobham Bridge. This view of* c.*1770 from Painshill shows the wooden bridge which was replaced in 1782.*

The increase in traffic on the Portsmouth Road brought prosperity to Street Cobham and inns and alehouses sprang up to cater for travellers. The chief inns were the *White Lion* (now *The Exchange*) and the *George*. The *George* was burnt down in the middle of the 19th century and replaced by the *Antelope*, which was demolished in the last century and replaced by the offices of Berkeley Homes. The *New and Complete English Traveller* of 1794 said, 'Cobham has many good inns, and is a clean flourishing place'. In the 1790s the *Ship Inn* had its name changed to the *Tartar* to commemorate HMS *Tartar*, a famous battleship of the time whose captain was Sir John Ross Lockhart. Although the *Tartar* has long since gone, this part of Cobham has been known as Tartar Hill. The passing traffic also provided employment for people like blacksmiths, wheelwrights and ostlers.

The Portsmouth Road was a much-used route and many famous people must have passed through this part of Cobham, including Lord Nelson. Jane Austen recorded in her diary how she broke her journey to Alton by stopping at Street Cobham, and John Wilkes, the politician and parliamentary reformer, stayed here on a number of occasions, either at the *White Lion* or the *George*. In the following century a local innkeeper, Robert Pitt, also became a partner in one of the stage-coach services that ran from London. The Red Rover ran from the *Bolt in Tun* in London to Southampton. A fellow partner in this enterprise was William Bennett, a Cobham farmer. The enterprising Pitt also ran a bus to Esher every Sunday and Monday morning in the summer to meet the first train from London.

Improved roads and increasing traffic also led to the rebuilding of Cobham's two bridges over the River Mole. An Act of Parliament was obtained for rebuilding the bridges at Cobham, Leatherhead and Godalming. Cobham Bridge, which had for so long been a source of contention between the respective lords of the manor, became a County Bridge and was rebuilt by George Gwilt in 1782. In 1787 he also rebuilt Downside Bridge.

During the latter part of the 18th century there were several abortive attempts to cut a canal across Cobham from the Tilt to Norwood Farm. In 1792, Major William Abington, who lived at Leigh Hill House (now the site of Leigh Place), headed local objections to a scheme that would have formed part of a navigable route from the Sussex coast to Dorking and then along the River Mole, to the Thames.

Cobham's Industrial Revolution

One Cobham resident with a special interest in improved roads and new canals was the entrepreneurial Alexander Raby, who brought the Industrial Revolution to Cobham when he developed an extensive centre for the production of iron goods at Downside. Downside Mill had long been used for the production of paper. In 1733, when it was in the possession of Richard Hinton, the mill was destroyed by fire and *Read's Weekly Journal* carried the following report:

> A few Days since a sad Accident happen'd near Cobham in Surrey, at Mr Hinton's Paper-Mill; Monday se'nnight his Pile of Faggots was burnt down, with his House, and Mill being on the opposite Side of the River, then escaped; but on the Thursday following the said Mill was set on fire and burnt to the Ground; there was near 200 pounds worth of Paper burnt, and the Mill lately

70   *Tinmans Row c.1910. These cottages were built by Alexander Raby to house his workers at Downside Mill.*

cost 600 pounds. The Man did not save any thing, he and his family narrowly escaping with their Lives. It is suspected that a Boy he had, did the horrid Deed; for tho' the Master of the Family did not save any Thing, yet the Boy removed his Cloathes, and laid them under a Hedge in a Field adjoining, and a Match and Tinder-Box was found therein. He denies the Fact strongly, but it's hoped this barbarous Piece of Villainy will be discovered.

On 15 May 1770 the mill was put up for auction at the *White Lion*, Cobham and subsequently purchased by Raby.

Alexander Raby came from a family of Wealden iron masters. He moved quickly to develop the site at Downside and purchased 52,000 bricks from Charles Hamilton of Painshill. A plan dating from about 1790 shows the site consisting of two water-powered machine shops, together with an iron foundry, a copper foundry and all the associated buildings. Unfortunately, nothing is known of the impact all this had upon the local community. At Coxes Lock near Weybridge, another of Raby's enterprises, he had installed a 'great hammer' nicknamed 'Hackering Jack' which delivered some 2,700 blows an hour. The noise was so great that local landowners and residents objected. Did the residents of Cobham have to suffer similar inconvenience?

There must have been a dramatic increase in the traffic on the local lanes as plant and raw material were delivered to Downside and the finished products taken away. The replacement of the old wooden bridge at Downside in 1787 would have been to Raby's great advantage and his personal interest in

71 *Cedar House, from a photograph taken* c.*1920 before the restoration carried out by Major Benton Fletcher.*

the provision of new and improved roads would no doubt have been heightened by his position as parish surveyor of highways. It seems more than likely that he had a personal interest in the plans for a canal through Cobham, part of the proposed route of which was across land either owned or rented.

But lack of indigenous raw materials and limitations on the site at Downside led the entrepreneurial Raby to take an interest in the developing coalfields of South Wales. In 1796 he took over an iron foundry and furnace at Llanelli. It was Raby's investment that encouraged Llanelli's development into the major industrial centre and port that it became in the 19th century. He eventually sold up at Downside but part of his legacy can still be seen in the row of cottages called Tinmans Row that he built for his workers in about 1804.

Other Trades, Industries and Occupations

Another small industry that developed in Cobham at this time was brick making, and small brick fields and kilns could be found in various parts of the parish. Thomas Page, lord of the manor, who lived at Pointers, was interested in the cultivation of furze for use in the burning of bricks and corresponded about this with Arthur Young in the 'Annals of Agriculture'. In the early part of the 18th century a glove maker living and working on River Hill was probably connected with the Fellmonger's Yard that was also to be found there.

72   *Cobham Mill from a watercolour of c.1809. This shows the mill that was demolished in 1953 to widen the road. (Private collection)*

Other industries more directly related to the land were those of brewing and milling. There appears to have been several small brewers in Cobham at one time but the end of the 18th century saw the establishment of a larger brewery at Street Cobham that ultimately became the Cobham Brewery. It stood on the Portsmouth Road opposite Wyndham Avenue. The Porter family, who figure prominently in 18th-century Cobham, were heavily involved in brewing and owned a number of the local inns and public houses. In the 1780s the brewer Joseph Moss came to live at Cedar House where he constructed a two-storey building for malting his own locally grown barley and a mill to crush the malt ready for transporting to his London brewery. Moss was in partnership with the Charrington brothers, who eventually took over the firm and made it into one of the largest breweries in the country. Hops were grown locally at Marsh Place (now Chestnut Lodge) and at Pointers.

One of the millers of corn at Cobham mill, Thomas Lucy, deserves a special mention in view of his questionable claim to the fortunes of the Lucy family of Charlecote Park near Stratford upon Avon. It is said the Lucys were so concerned at the possible authenticity of the claim that they made Thomas a substantial pay-off which enabled him to purchase both the freehold of the mill and the neighbouring Old Meadow in November 1778 for the sum of £1,050. In 1799 Cobham mill, then in the occupation of John Tupper, was washed away in a severe flood. The property was quickly rebuilt and, in the 1820s, enlarged by the addition of another mill. The older building was demolished for road widening in 1953 and it is the 19th-century addition that today is Cobham's best known landmark.

Windmills were once a common feature of the Surrey landscape. One stood on the edge of the Fairmile Common, near the present *Fairmile Hotel*. In 1815 James Thorpe was the miller and in 1851 Thomas Bowel was working the mill with one assistant.

Painshill Park

With its ease of access to London, Cobham was an ideal place in which to have a country estate. Without a doubt, the most important local estate and the greatest attraction in 18th-century Cobham was that at Painshill, with its famous landscape garden created by the Hon. Charles Hamilton. Although most of the estate was in the neighbouring parish of Walton on Thames, it spilled over into Cobham and was, and still is, referred to as Painshill, Cobham.

Charles Hamilton was the youngest son of James, 6th Earl of Abercorn. Following his education at Westminster School and Christchurch, Oxford, Hamilton went on the Grand Tour of Europe first in 1725 and then again in 1732. In Italy he made friends with many of the leading patrician families and spent time collecting antiquities and pictures that he sent home. On his return to England, Hamilton found employment in the household of Frederick, Prince of Wales, who was then living at Kew. Looking for an estate nearby, he found and purchased the land at Painshill. Members of the Fox family, who owned Downe Place, may have influenced his choice of Cobham. Hamilton seems to have acquired the estate from William Bellamy, a wealthy and successful barrister. He extended Bellamy's estate by lease and purchase to create his masterpiece. In order to finance the work, he was forced to borrow heavily from his friend Henry Fox, later Lord Holland.

73 *Painshill House from an engraving of 1787.*

74   *The Hon. Charles Hamilton, painted on the Grand Tour by David in 1732.*

75   *Painshill: the Gothick Pavilion from an early 19th-century engraving by Prosser.*

Horace Walpole later described the land that Hamilton acquired as 'a cursed hill', and it was mostly heath land. There were two or three small farms within the estate whose histories could be traced back for several centuries. Bellamy probably merged them into one holding, having purchased the estate from Gabriel, Marquis De Quesne, a colourful Frenchman of noble ancestry whose grandfather had been one of France's most famous admirals. De Quesne in turns seems to have purchased the estate from the Smyther family who also owned Downe Place. De Quesne probably laid out a small formal park at Painshill and built the house that became Hamilton's residence.

Landscape gardeners such as William Kent were also active at this time but, whereas they sought to improve the natural landscape through the creation of theatrical set pieces and eye catchers, Hamilton's masterpiece was created from scratch. Based upon paintings he had seen on the Grand Tour, Hamilton's three dimensional canvas was one into which the admirer might step and explore. Just ten years after he acquired it, Hamilton's park had become famous throughout the country and visitors, always welcome, flocked to see it. Painshill became an additional source of revenue for local innkeepers, as the following extract from Manning and Bray's *History of Surrey* records: 'Mr Hamilton indulged the publick with the sight of its [Painshill's] beauties, and even allowed the use of low chairs drawn by small horses which were provided at the inns of Cobham, to which the excursion of numerous summer parties was a source of considerable emolument.'

William Bray, the Surrey historian, came to Painshill in 1797 and John Wesley, founder of Methodism, visited on at least three occasions and recorded his impressions in his *Journal*. Horace Walpole, another visitor, wrote, 'All is great and foreign and rude; the walks seem not designed but cut through the woods of pines; and the style of the whole is so grand, and conducted with so serious an air of wild and uncultivated extent, that when you look down on this seeming forest, you are amazed to find it contains a very few acres.' The poet Thomas Gray came to Painshill in 1754 and wrote of 'Mr Hamilton's at Cobham ... which all the world talks of and I have seen seven years ago.'

The painter Francis Nicholson came and sketched, and two American presidents, Thomas Jefferson and John Adams, visited the park. John Wilkes, the parliamentary reformer, recorded in his diary how he 'sauntered through the Elysium of Mr Hamilton's gardens 'til eight in the evening like the first solitary man through Paradise'.

Hamilton shifted enormous amounts of soil to create a lake surrounded by steep terrain, some of which was planted to resemble Alpine scenery. The lake was eventually extended to 20 acres and was designed so that it should never be seen all at once, thus deceiving the visitor into thinking it was even larger. A number of decorative bridges were constructed giving access to islands in the lake and to the centrepiece of the park, the Grotto, a magical cavern constructed in brick and plaster and decorated with crystals and artificial stalactites. In another part of the park was the Hermitage, a building of rustic appearance made from logs and roots. This was the home of the almost legendary hermit employed by

Hamilton at a reputedly enormous salary, whose conditions of employment were said to include silence at all times. In addition he was to wear 'a camlet robe', use an hourglass for his timepiece, never trim his beard and nails, and nor was he to stray from the park. The legend states that the unfortunate man was not suited to the solitary life and was discovered after only a few weeks supping ale in a local public house!

One writer has commented that Painshill was a garden whose mood changed from one part of the park to another. The effect was helped by other follies such as the Temple of Bacchus, the Roman Mausoleum, a Turkish Tent, a medieval watchtower and a pretty Gothick pavilion, perched on a hill overlooking the lake, which drew scorn from Horace Walpole; he wrote, 'the Goths never built summer houses'. A later addition was the façade of a ruined Gothick Abbey which Hamilton constructed to hide the remains of a tile works he had developed to help finance his project.

Hamilton was also a keen arboriculturist, and many of the trees he planted had been imported from overseas. Some of the earliest rhododendrons to be grown in this country were planted at Painshill and the great cedars of Lebanon, now so much a feature of the park, include one that is believed to be the largest in Europe. Hamilton needed to finance his park-making and his commercial brick and tile works venture already mentioned. He also planted a vineyard that produced a white sparkling wine of sufficient quality to deceive the French Ambassador into believing it was champagne. William Cobbett recorded having visited the vineyard when he was a child.

76 *View from the Temple of Bacchus by the Swedish artist Elias Martin.*

Hamilton's house, of which only a fragment now remains, stood near the Portsmouth Road, on the brow of the hill, and was probably an enlargement of the house constructed by De Quesne. The present house was built by Benjamin Bond Hopkins, who purchased the estate in 1773 when Hamilton retired to Bath to continue his landscaping activities from a house in the fashionable Royal Crescent. Bond Hopkins' architect was Richard Jupp who created a simple but elegant two-storeyed villa of five bays with a large porch of four composite columns to the east and a bow to the west. Single-storeyed colonnaded wings originally extended either side of the house. Sadly, the house was altered and enlarged several times during the 19th century by architects such as

Decimus Burton and Richard Norman Shaw, who removed the original portico. Painshill Park is now one of the nation's great garden restoration success stories and the public again have the opportunity to lose themselves in Charles Hamilton's earthly paradise.

Cobham Park
Cobham's other 'big house' was Cobham Park. This estate was formed from the purchase and merger of several small farms and land holdings that included Downe Place, the ancient home to the Downe family, which in 1671 had passed to George Smyther, a nephew of John Downe. In 1708 Frances, Viscountess Lanesborough of Bishop's Manor, East Horsley, purchased the manor of Cobham from Robert Gavell and his son and heir

apparent, Robert Gavell junior. The purchase excluded Cobham Court Farm but included a property called Bridge House Farm that stood on the site of the present Cobham Park.

In 1720 Lady Lanesborough purchased from the Smyther family 'the capital messuage called Downe place alias Downe Hall and all barns land belonging – containing 140 acres in Cobham, and Little Bookham Common Surrey in the tenure of John Box'. In that same year her solicitor wrote that *'she had found great benefit by the country ayre and that her health is much improved.'* Sadly the benefits were short-lived and Lady Lanesborough died the following year leaving both the manor of Cobham and Downe Place to her grandsons of the Fox family.

In 1728 James Fox, of East Horsley, sold Bridge House Farm, described as 'a very old house and out houses frequently out of repair, which occasion a considerable expense to repair them', to John Bridges of Cobham for £1,000. Soon after completing his purchase, Bridges set about building a splendid new mansion in the classical style on the site of farm. It has been suggested that Roger Morris, an influential architect of the time, may have designed the building that was said to have been based on Palladio's designs for his Villa Zeno. Little is known of John Bridges, although he may have been connected to the family of the same name who owned Ember Court near Esher. His will shows a relationship to the family of Sir Brook Bridges of Goodnestone in Kent, to whom he left most of his estate. There is a connection here with Jane Austen, whose brother Edward married Sir Brook's daughter Elizabeth. Elizabeth and her brothers and sisters also benefited under John Bridge's will.

77 *Cobham Park from the drawing by William Porden c.1815. This was the house built by John Bridges on the site of Bridge House Farm. It is now the site of the present Cobham Park mansion. (British Library)*

78 *Sir John, later Lord Ligonier, from a contemporary engraving.*

The house that John Bridges built was very grand and described in Daniel Defoe's *A Tour Through The Whole Island of Great Britain* as follows:

79 *Edward Ligonier from the portrait by Gainsborough (1770).*

80 *Penelope Ligonier from the portrait by Gainsborough (1770).*

The Apartments within seem very commodious and the principal rooms are elegantly fitted up, the ceilings being gilt, and all the Members are richly ornamented. The Offices below are very conveniently and judiciously contrived to answer the purposes for which they were designed. But what chiefly struck my Curiosity on seeing it was a false Storey contrived on each side of the House, taken from the Difference in the Height of the side-rooms, from those Principal Apartments: and these are converted into long galleries with a small Apartment at one end, which affords a communication between them. In the Attick Story there are very good Lodging-rooms, which are well laid together: so that for the size of this House, there is hardly any other near London, which has more useful and elegant Apartments.

The account continues with a description of the grounds, which had been partially landscaped: The river had been widened in places and the excavated soil use to create 'a natural slope, with a broad Grass-walk, planted with sweet Shrubs on each side: and at the End of the Walk is a fine Room, which has a view of the Water lengthwise, and is a sweet retreat in hot weather'.

In 1749 John Bridges sold Bridge House Farm 'together with the Capital Messuage or Mansion lately erected thereon by the said John Bridges' to The Honourable Sir John Ligonier, a colourful military character of Huguenot descent. Born in Provence,

Ligonier had fought under Marlborough at Blenheim and subsequently rose to become Commander in Chief of the British Army in 1757. He took part in no fewer than 23 general actions and 19 sieges without receiving a wound. Ligonier's guests at Cobham included William Pitt the elder and, while the house was chiefly a place of retreat and leisure, in 1759 it became his headquarters when laying out a military camp on Send Heath near Woking.

In 1759 Ligonier, then described as 'The Right Honourable John Lord Viscount Ligonier in the Kingdom of Ireland Field Marshall [*sic*] and Commander in Chief of His Majesty's forces and Knight of the Most Honourable Order of the Bath', purchased Downe Place, together with 150 acres of land in Cobham and Little Bookham, from James Fox. He then merged the two properties to form Cobham Park. It seems likely that the old Downe Place mansion was demolished and the new house built by John Bridges took its place as the chief house.

Ligonier continued to enlarge and improve the estate during his lifetime and, although much of it was spent in London, he loved to come down to Cobham where he could entertain his friends. Although always very popular with the ladies, Ligonier never married. He is reputed to have had four mistresses, whose combined age did not exceed 58 years and he also formed a long and lasting attachment to Lady Mary Campbell, who often stayed with him at Cobham.

Lord Ligonier died in 1770, aged 89, was buried in Cobham church, and his monument was erected in Westminster Abbey. He was succeeded by his nephew Edward who, in

81 The Stable Adventure, or the Luckey Expedient, *a satirical cartoon of Lady Ligonier and the stable boy at Cobham Park (1772).*

the following year, divorced his wife Penelope after fighting a sword duel in Hyde Park with her lover, Count Vittorio Alfieri, Italy's national poet. The story of their relationship became a *cause célèbre* in its day. Lady Ligonier was described as a classic example of depravity and it was written of her that she was 'a Lady so Dove-like in the Temper of her Constitution that she granted without the Preliminaries of Entreaty, every Indulgence which the most lawless inclination could suggest'. As well as her much publicised affair with the Count, Lady Ligonier further embarrassed her husband and scandalised polite society by having an affair with a stable boy at Cobham Park. Needless to say, Alfieri's ego was also severely dented by this disclosure.

After many years in the hands of trustees, the estate was purchased by General Henry Lawes Luttrell, 2nd Earl of Carhampton and Colonel of the 6th Regiment of Dragoon Guards. His wife Jane was considered to be one of the most beautiful women of her time. In 1804 the Carhamptons moved to Painshill, and two years later Harvey Christian Combe purchased Downe Place for the sum of £30,000. Combe had made his money in

82 *Harvey Christian Combe from a contemporary engraving.*

porter brewing, was a close friend of both the Prince of Wales and Charles James Fox, and had been Lord Mayor of London in 1799 and MP for the City in 1802. Combe continued the policy of enlarging and improving the park, and a bill of 1807 from his lawyer refers to work done in connection with 'Having two Publick Highways in your Grounds diverted and turned thro' other parts thereof and a footpath stopped up'. Harvey Combe died at Cobham in 1818 leaving an estate worth £200,000. He was buried in the large family mausoleum in St Andrew's churchyard. The architect of this monument seems to have been heavily influenced by Sir John Soane. Combe's descendants were to play a very prominent part in Cobham and its affairs in the 19th century when they became acknowledged as the local squires.

When James Fox sold Bridge House Farm and Downe Place he retained the lordship of the manor, and this eventually passed to his nephew, also named James, when he was only four years old. James junior's uncle, George Fox-Lane, ran the estate for his nephew, but died when his ward was only 17 years old. The young James did not take his responsibilities seriously, fell into bad company and started to gamble away his inheritance. In 1776 he narrowly avoided imprisonment for debts and was packed off on the Grand Tour with his tutor. Whilst on his way to Italy, however, James managed to escape from his tutor and returned to Paris where he continued to gamble. It was in Paris that he met Robert Mackreth, a notorious swindler of the day, who made his fortune by preying on young men such as James Fox. Fox was forced to sell his estates and Mackreth became a trustee for the sale, but in 1799 he bought the estates himself and, before completion of the contract, sold the Cobham estate at a highly advanced price to Thomas Page who lived at Pointers, Downside.

Pointers

When Thomas Page purchased the manor, Pointers, a large old house in the south of the parish, became the manor house. Page had inherited the property from his father, and following his acquisition of the manor he made considerable changes to the property, enlarging it and moving the public highway which passed between the house and the river to the other side of the house, thus providing himself with more privacy and a superb river frontage. Page married Catherine Brooksbank, who brought to the marriage a considerable fortune of over £11,000 in stocks and shares,

83 *Pointers from the 1822 watercolour by J. Hassell. (Private Collection)*

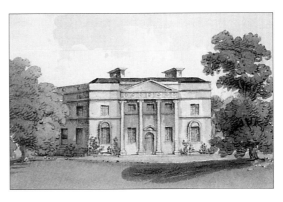

84 *Hatchford House from the 1822 watercolour by J. Hassell. (Surrey History Centre)*

and at Pointers they entertained several members of the royal family including the Duke of York, who lived at nearby Oatlands. When Page died in 1842 he left his estates together with the manor of Cobham to his daughter and sole heir, Sophia Catherine.

Hatchford Park

Adjoining the Pointers estate was Hatchford Park, another of Cobham's important houses in the 18th century. The property had belonged to John Wilson, an insurance broker who on his death left to his wife Elizabeth an annuity to be paid by the Mercers' Company, together with 'all my household goods, plat, linen, pictures, rings, watch, carriages of all kinds, and horses, and wearing apparel, at my house at Hatchford Farm and my house in the City of London and elsewhere'. To his son John junior he left the estate with the proviso that his widow was to have the use of the house at Hatchford.

John Lewin Smith, who purchased the estate from John Wilson junior, rebuilt Hatchford Park in 1774. In 1778 Smith was appointed Sheriff of Surrey and four years later he sold the estate to Benjamin Brooks-

bank, whose daughter had married Thomas Page. Brooksbank later sold the Hatchford estate to Andrew Ramsay, who afterwards assumed the name of Ramsay Karr. Ramsay had served as Acting Governor of Bombay for eight months before retiring to Hatchford where he died in 1799.

In 1802 the estate was purchased by Miss Isabella Saltonstall who moved here from Rose Lodge in Cobham. Isabella was a wealthy heiress and a patron of the artist George Stubbs. She had a collection of his pictures and was featured as the character of Una in Stubbs's painting based upon Spenser's *Fairie Queene*. When Isabella Saltonstall died her estate was worth in the region of £45,000, a considerable sum for those days. In her will she remembered the poor of Cobham and her bequest now forms part of Cobham Combined Charities.

Other Houses

Just as the bigger houses of Cobham were being rebuilt at this time, the owners of smaller properties were also keen to keep up appearances, and several old houses rebuilt at this time included Cobham Court, Lime

House in Church Street, and Chasemore Farm at Downside. It is also likely that Ham Manor, a textbook example of early 18th-century architecture, replaced an earlier house. Rather than rebuild, many property owners chose the cheaper option of encasing their old timber-framed houses and cottages in brick. Several Cobham houses were thus improved and examples that can be seen today include Cedar House, the Old Mill House, the former *White Lion* at Street Cobham and Pyports, opposite St Andrew's church. The latter was the home of the Freeland family during the last half of the 18th century.

The Freelands had moved to Cobham from Ockham in the 17th century. Jeremiah Freeland took over Marsh Place Farm, now Chestnut Lodge, by the Old Common, and it was his son John who purchased Pyports in 1761. John Freeland came from a family of yeoman farmers but rose to become a country gentleman. He married a wealthy wife and found good husbands for his daughters, one of whom married Harry Charrington the

brewer. Prior to the Freeland family's occupation, Pyports had been home to the Skrine family and Henry Skrine 'The Tourist', a well-known topographical writer, was probably born at the house.

In 1798 John Freeland insured Pyports and Marsh Place with the Sun Insurance Company. It was the practice of insurance companies at this time to place firemarks carrying their symbol on the exterior of the property accompanied by the policy number. The purpose of these plaques was to be a guide to the fire fighters, each company having its own brigade. It has been said that if a building caught fire and the brigade arriving on the scene found the house was not insured with their company they would go home! These 'fire marks' can often still be seen on old buildings and other Cobham examples can be seen at the Old Mill House and Pointers Farm Cottage near Halfpenny Cross.

Overbye in Church Street was built at the beginning of the century, and on the other side of the churchyard is Church Gate House,

85 & 86 *Ham Manor (left) from the watercolour by J. Hassell. Ham Manor is one of Surrey's finest early 18th-century houses (Surrey History Service) and Pyports (right) from the 1822 watercolour by J. Hassell (British Library).*

87 *John and Lydia Freeland of Pyports. (Private Collection)*

88 *Henry Skrine (later known as 'Mr Skrine the Tourist'). Skrine spent his early years at Pyports.*

which dates from about 1760. There was also development at Street Cobham on the increasingly busy Portsmouth Road, and the elegant houses now known as Old House and Vine House were built, probably by Benjamin Bond Hopkins of Painshill, towards the end of the century.

During the second half of the 18th century there was an increase in speculative building of suitable homes. The small red-bricked cottages that once stood either side of River Hill dated from this time and there were similar developments on the Portsmouth Road. An important survivor from this time is 5 Church Street ('Phoenix') that has retained its original 18th-century façade.

One of Cobham's better-known trades-men at this time was Uriah Collyer. In addition to being both carpenter and builder,

89 *Old House and Vine House, Portsmouth Road from a photograph taken* c.*1920.*

90 *River Hill in the late 19th century, showing the small 18th-century cottages that stood on either side of the road. All the cottages were demolished when the road was widened in the 1960s.*

91 *The* Running Mare, *Cobham Tilt, c.1935. The name of the pub is a reminder of the horse racing that took place here in the 18th century.*

Collyer was a surveyor able to turn his hand to the drawing of maps and plans such as the one he made for the proposed enclosure of Breach Hill (now known as Chatley Heath) that can now be seen in the Surrey History Centre. He lived in the house now called Millwater Cottage which stands opposite Cobham Mill, and his yard (now Skilton's yard) adjoined it. Although most of the buildings on this site date from the 19th century, it is unusual to find a site used for the same purpose for over two hundred years.

In 1794 Collyer was called upon by William Bray, Steward of the Manor, to prepare a report and valuation of the property which stood at the junction of Church Street and High Street. The following extract provides an interesting glimpse of what a shop keeper's premises were like at this time:

A brick built House with Kitchen, Parlour, Shop & Bake House on the Ground Floor, and four Chambers above. With Stable & Cart House and Hayloft over both Stables and Carthouse. And Building adjoining to the same used as a Brewhouse But now connected to a Weavers Shop with Dungyard, Court before the house, & Passage behind the above described Stable & Weavers Shop leading to the Privy and Turf House at the North end of the Stable.

Nonconformity

Cobham's reputation as a centre of nonconformity was helped in the 18th century by the rise of the new independent tradesmen and landless artisans. Although Wesley visited Cobham on several occasions, there is no record of his ever having preached in the village. It was not until the middle years of the following century that Methodism was

92 *Francis Wrangham, Curate of Cobham and friend of William Wordsworth.*

to become established locally. However, it is likely that Cobham people would have travelled to hear Wesley at nearby Leatherhead where he preached his last indoor sermon. The denomination that did find a warm response in Cobham was the Independents or Congregationalists. In 1764 and 1767 a building near the junction of Downside Road and Plough Lane was registered by them for worship.

Leisure and Sport

Horse racing and cricket are first recorded in Cobham in the 18th century. Horse racing took place on the old Tilt Green and several of the races here were recorded in the racing calendars of the time. It is likely that the *Running Mare* pub took its name from its proximity to the race course. On 24 August

1771 the *Gazetteer & London Daily Advertiser* reported, 'On Monday next will be played on Cobham-tilt, the second great cricket match for £20, between the Earl of Tankerville and the Cobham-club, who won the first match, with only three wickets down, in their last hands.' The Earl of Tankerville who lived at Mount Felix, Walton on Thames, helped establish the rules for modern cricket in 1774. One Cobham resident who enjoyed playing cricket was iron master Alexander Raby. In his old age he wrote to an acquaintance in Cobham stating, 'I am as well as ever tho I cannot run as fast nor jump as high as when Ld. Tankerville, Sir Francis Vincent, his brother and we used to play at Cricket upon the Tilt 50 years ago.'

William Wordsworth and the Cobham Curate

In the closing years of the 18th century William Wordsworth frequently came to Cobham to visit his old friend Francis Wrangham, who served as curate at St Andrew's church in 1794-5. Wrangham was a classical scholar from Cambridge who had been excluded from a fellowship at Trinity Hall in 1793 on account of his liberal opinions. He presumably took the curacy at Cobham to provide an income but it was supplemented by tutoring pupils with his friend Basil Montague. Exactly where they held the school is not known, although a 'Churchyard Foundation School' was held in part of Church Stile House in the early years of the following century.

Wordsworth's great friend Coleridge is known to have visited Josiah Wedgwood II, who lived at Stoke D'Abernon Manor House between 1795 and 1800.

Nine

THE NINETEENTH CENTURY

A sequestered country hamlet

In 1801 Cobham was still a small rural community with a population of 1,200, one fifth of whom were engaged in agriculture. The total number of occupied houses in the village was only 208. By 1901 the population had risen to almost 3,900, with 797 inhabited houses. The century was one of great change both nationally and locally. In Cobham, as in other places close to London, much of the farmland began to be replaced by low-cost housing development and gradually the separate communities of Street Cobham, Church Cobham and Tilt Cobham merged into one.

93 *Cobham High Street from the 1822 watercolour by J. Hassell. (British Library) This view should be compared with that facing the title page.*

The sweeping agricultural changes of the previous century had already led to the establishment of several compact estates and farms such as Cobham Park, Cobham Court, Eaton Farm, Fairmile Farm and Leigh Hill Farm. A guide book of the 1840s described Cobham as 'quite a model of a sequestered country hamlet which must be very refreshing in its quietness to the many anglers who escape to it from the noise of London'. A number of interesting, wealthy and colourful personalities chose to make their homes in the village either in existing properties or in newly built villa residences.

Brook Farm and the Moore family

One of the first of the new houses to appear in 19th-century Cobham was Brook Farm, built by Colonel Edward Letherland in 1801 on land lately enclosed from the Tilt Common. In 1804 he sold the property to Admiral Sir Graham Moore, who in that same year had enriched himself with prize money from Spanish treasure ships captured off Cadiz in the Peninsular Wars. The sale particulars described Brook Farm as 'a desirable freehold estate comprising as singularly elegant villa with roomy stabling … suited to the Villa, the Mansion or the Farm Ornee'. Graham Moore's fame was

94 *Brook Farm from the 1822 watercolour by J. Hassell. (British Library)*

95 *Admiral Sir Graham Moore of Brook Farm, Cobham from the portrait painted by Sir Thomas Lawrence in 1792. (National Portrait Gallery)*

eclipsed by that of his brother Sir John, who died a hero's death at the Battle of Coruña. Sir John often visited his brother at Cobham and in 1807 planted the oak tree that still stands in the garden of one of the houses in Oak Road. Admiral Moore spent a good deal of time and money on his Cobham home and in 1825 he recorded in his *Journal*, 'In fine weather, and particularly in the early spring of the year, this place appears very beautiful in my eyes.' Brook Farm was eventually demolished in about 1926 and Brook Farm Road and Oak Road now cover the estate.

Other Naval Connections

Another distinguished naval personage, and a friend of Graham Moore, was Sir William Hoste, who came to spend his retirement at Pyports, opposite the parish church, in about 1826. Early in his career Hoste became known as 'the young Nelson' because he had served under the great admiral for five years and was present at the Battle of the Nile. Hoste regretted that he had missed Trafalgar and later wrote, 'not to have been in the battle is enough to make one mad; but to have lost such a friend [Nelson] besides is really sufficient to almost overwhelm me.' At Cobham Hoste became an enthusiastic gardener, taking a particular interest in flowers. He died in London in 1828 and his monument is in St Paul's Cathedral.

The tall brick tower on Chatley Heath at this time formed part of the chain of semaphore towers linking Portsmouth with the Admiralty in London. The master station at Portsmouth kept in touch with ships in the harbour by a signalling system not unlike that once used on the railways. The chain of

96   Captain Sir William Hoste of Pyports.

97   The Semaphore Tower on Chatley Heath in 1823 from the watercolour by J. Hassell. (Private Collection)

towers was constructed in the 1820s at intervals of between five and ten miles on vantage points such as Pewley Down in Guildford, Telegraph Hill at Hinchley Wood and Putney Heath. The system was replaced in 1847 by the electric telegraph. The tower, which is featured in a novel called *The Woman at the Door* by Warwick Deeping (1937), became a private home for some while. Surrey County Council have restored this unique piece of history to working order and now own it.

Heywood and a Royal Romance

Heywood stands at the back of the Fairmile Common and is now the home of the International Community School. In the late 18th century the estate was called 'The Hermitage' and was the property of John

Cambel. The present house dates from about 1804, when it was rebuilt by Dr William Anderson, who later built what is now the *Fairmile Hotel*. In 1820 Dr Anderson sold the property to Prince Leopold of Saxe Coburg, widower of Princess Charlotte, daughter of George IV, who had died in childbirth at nearby Claremont. Charlotte's death left Leopold heartbroken and the nation in mourning. Leopold was later introduced to Karoline Bauer, a German actress who bore a remarkable resemblance to his late wife, but since marriage would have cost him his pension of £50,000 a year as widower of the Princess Royal, she was secretly installed in a house in Regent's Park. Some sort of marriage was arranged in 1829, and on New Year's Eve Karoline and her mother were moved to Heywood.

98   *Caroline Bauer.*

her mother were allowed to return to their native Germany. Karoline drew from Her Majesty's Treasury a pension settled upon her by Leopold for the remainder of her life.

Upper Court and the Brothertons

A short way from Heywood, along the Portsmouth Road towards Esher, is a house called Upper Court. Originally known as The Firs, it was built in 1846 by General Sir Thomas William Brotherton GCB, aide-de-camp to William IV, on a piece of land formerly known as Dog Kennel Field. Brotherton was a veteran of the Napoleonic Wars and one of the most distinguished military men of his day. He seems to have been present at almost every significant military engagement during the Peninsular War. At one stage he was taken prisoner by the French and later released by way of exchange.

Painshill House

In the early years of the 19th century the noted architect Decimus Burton was called in to make a number of alterations and additions to Painshill House. In the 1880s another owner, Charles James Leaf, commissioned Richard Norman Shaw to design a large pseudo-Tudor house in Victorian baronial style. Fortunately Shaw's plans were not executed, and all he seems to have done is create a service wing on one side and make additions to the lodges. The removal of the great portico may have also have been his doing; a simple wooden veranda that was hardly in keeping with the classical proportions of Richard Jupp's designs replaced it. This veranda was in turn replaced in the 1920s by the present portico,

Unfortunately Karoline hated her secluded life at Heywood, which she considered to be 'the most dismal place conceivable; musty rooms, brown wall paper and faded curtains within, and a weed-chocked part without. High fir trees pressed round so closely as to keep out the sun; nothing could be seen from the windows; not a sound was to be heard.'

On one occasion Karoline and her mother were allowed to visit the grounds of Claremont where they encountered the Duchess of Kent with her little daughter, the future Queen Victoria. It was therefore probably something of a relief to all concerned when Leopold was offered first the throne of Greece, which he declined, and then of Belgium, which he accepted. Karoline and that was removed from the Temple of Bacchus in the park. Robert Adam made a number of designs for the ceiling of the Temple and he may be responsible for the whole building, including the portico.

The Painshill estate passed through a succession of owners in the 19th century, including the Earl of Carhampton, who moved there from Cobham Park, W.H. Cooper, who was High Sheriff of Surrey, and Charles James Leaf, a city merchant and philanthropist whose friend, the poet Matthew Arnold, came to live on the estate. Leaf's son Walter was a member of the Cambridge Apostles. He had won a classical scholarship to Trinity College and later went on to distinguish himself in the banking world. In 1926, as President of the International Chamber of Commerce, he made an important and successful visit to Germany with a view to economic reconciliation. However Walter Leaf's reputation rests chiefly on his work as a Greek scholar: he collaborated with Andrew Lang to produce a translation of Homer's *Iliad*. He published a number of other books and later he and his wife became close friends of Virginia Woolf.

Painshill eventually passed into the ownership of the Combe family. Some of Cobham's older residents can still recall visits there for Sunday School treats and Empire Day sports, when Mrs Combe was in residence.

Cobham Lodge and Caroline Molesworth

To the south of Cobham stands Cobham Lodge, a delightful, elegant Georgian property built in about 1803-4 for Colonel Joseph Hardy to the designs of J.B. Papworth

99 *Painshill House in 1822 from the watercolour by J. Hassell.(Private Collection)*

100 *Cobham Lodge from a photograph taken* c.*1910.*

101 *The old Cobham Park from a mid-19th-century photograph.*

on land belonging to Lord Carhampton. In 1823 the young Caroline Molesworth came to live here. Her mother was the widow of Sir William Molesworth of Pencarrow, Cornwall. Lady Molesworth had inherited the Cobham house from General Felix Buckley, a veteran of the Battle of Culloden, who had purchased it from Joseph Hardy. Caroline continued to live there after her mother's death in 1842 and until her own in 1872. During this time she kept a comprehensive account of the meteorology, flora, fauna and natural phenomena of the district. The notes were published after her death as *The Cobham Journals*. Although much of the information is of a scientific nature, there are reference to local events, such as 'a peculiar vibration, believed to be an earthquake' in 1830. In 1840 'a hurricane … blowing down trees at Cobham Park and Painshill' is recorded, and later there are references to wild geese, snipe, red-throated diver and great crested grebe being seen in the vicinity and to 'a bittern shot in Cobham Park'. Caroline Molesworth was noted for her kindness and generosity and 'with a character for eccentricity not wholly unmerited, she was still greatly respected in her own neighbourhood.'

Cobham Park and the Combe family

In 1806 Downe Place, as it was then known, was purchased by Harvey Christian Combe from Lord Carhampton, who then moved to Painshill. Combe acquired an interest in the Woodyard Brewery in London's Long Acre in 1787 and went into the highly profitable business of porter brewing. He became one of the most successful brewers of the time, a respected public figure, a fearless orator and a patron of the arts. He was greatly respected by the royal family, and in 1800, as Lord Mayor of London, he bestowed the honours of the City on Admiral Horatio Nelson. Combe employed the architect J.B. Papworth to make alterations to his Cobham residence and Brayley's *History of Surrey* described it as 'a handsome and substantial building, nearly square, with a neat portico erected in place of a veranda. The good saloon, with coved and ornamented ceiling, was turned into a billiard room, and the other convenient apartments were embellished with busts and pictures.'

Cobham was dominated throughout the 19th century by those who owned the land and it was Harvey Combe's son, also named Harvey, who, upon inheriting the estate from his father, set about improving and enlarging it. By careful purchase, consolidation and improvement of land, Harvey junior created an estate worthy of his wealth and standing. It was he who gave Cobham Park and the surrounding area much of the appearance it still has today. He was at one time Master of the Old Berkley Hunt and had the unusual distinction of having a railway locomotive named after him. The engine was used in the construction of the London and Birmingham Railway in 1836-7.

102 *Cobham Park in the 1880s.*

A poem in *The Monthly Magazine* of 1834 contains the following reference to Cobham Park:

Let lofty mansions great men keep –
I have no wish to rob 'em –
Not courtly Claremont, Esher's steep,
Nor Squire Combe's at Cobham.

Manorial records of the 1820s reveal that Harvey junior was pursuing a policy of buying up old and dilapidated farms and cottages in the Downside area. Although these were copyhold and occupied by manorial tenants, upon payment of a small fine Combe was allowed to demolish them. One such property was the 'Old Garden House' which stood opposite the entrance to Cobham Park, on the site of the present Cobham Park Gardens. John Hassell's view of this building in 1822 shows it with a prominent brick gable in the Dutch style that was popular in the 17th century. In the 1680s it had been the home

of Robert Burgess, a blacksmith, but by 1797 it was occupied by Thomas Bullin, a 'seedsman' who had a shop here. The fact that the site is used today for the cultivation and sale of plants shows a rare continuity of use over a period of at least 200 years.

Many of the local people who depended upon such smallholdings must have been very unsettled by what was happening, but Combe quickly replaced the demolished cottages with model estate workers cottages which can still be seen today around Downside Common, a visible legacy of his desire to improve the living conditions of his tenants. In addition, he brought fresh water to Downside by providing the village pump which still stands next to St Michael's chapel. Sadly, Combe died before the project was completed and it was left to his sister to finish the job.

Harvey's sister, Mary Anne, also provided Cobham with new school buildings in Cedar

Road. These were completed and opened in 1860 in memory of her late brother and replaced the parish school room built on the Tilt in 1839. The buildings remained functioning as a school until the 1970s.

Harvey Combe junior's death in 1857 resulted in the sale of his famous herd of Shorthorn cattle at Downside Farm that raised upwards of £5,000. He was succeeded by his nephew Charles, who rebuilt the old Cobham Park after it was partly destroyed by fire in the early 1870s. The new house, completed in 1873, is built of Bargate and Portland stone to the designs of Edward Middleton Barry RA, third son of Sir Charles Barry, architect of the Palace of Westminster and *Charing Cross Hotel*. Cobham Park cost £26,000 to build and was provided with all the latest amenities. It is reputed to have been the third house in the country to have electricity, a generator wheel having been installed at Downside Mill which had been purchased by Combe in 1865. Another small wheel was installed in the Park in 1884 by Whitmore and Binyon of Wickham Market, Suffolk, to bring water to the house. Elsewhere in the grounds there was an icehouse which, when filled with ice from the lake in winter and packed in with straw, would stay cold throughout the summer.

Much of the original decoration of Cobham Park remains although the house is currently being converted into luxury apartments. In the entrance hall, the large oak mantelpiece is enriched by a square panel carved with the Combe coat-of-arms impaling Inglis (Mrs Combe's family). Two carved heads either side of the fireplace are said to represent Charles and his wife in medieval dress. The house formerly contained a number of family portraits and marble statues of members of the family by Queen Victoria's favourite sculptor, F.J. Williamson, who lived at Esher.

Regular visitors to Squire Combe and his family at the Park included the poet Matthew Arnold, who also lived in Cobham, and Rosa Lewis, the famous 'Duchess of Duke Street', a friend of Combe's valet. A tragedy occurred in the early part of the 19th century when one of the gamekeepers was shot dead by poachers and the routine of life in a country house was again disturbed in 1925 when the butler committed suicide with his master's revolver.

One of Charles Combe's special interests was the breeding of racehorses and he helped establish the Cobham Stud Company on a site on the Downside Road that had formerly been the site of the *Waggon and Horses* alehouse. The fortunes of the Stud were built on a famous stallion called Blair Athol, 'the Blaze-faced King of Cobham' which was purchased for £13,000. In the course of his life the horse produced no fewer than 60 yearlings, and in the 1896 Derby five of the runners were his progeny. In 1896 the Cobham Parish Magazine reported that the annual sale of yearlings at the Stud meant 'a special train down from town for the occasion, and this was fairly well filled but apparently most of the travellers went in for the inspection and free lunch rather than for the business in as much as there were very few purchasers'. According to the autobiography of William Allison, the Stud manager, this particular sale brought to Cobham HRH The Prince of Wales, later Edward VII, accompanied by his mistress Lillie Langtry.

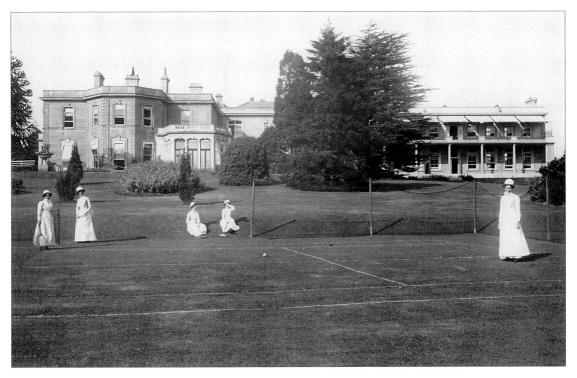

103 *Knowle Hill Park after it became the Schiff Home of Recovery.*

The Development of Cobham Fairmile

Whilst Cobham Park and its estate were being enlarged, another of Cobham's big estates, the Fairmile Farm estate which had once extended from the old Portsmouth Road across to the parish boundary with Stoke D'Abernon, was being broken up. John Earley Cook, who owned the brickfields at Oxshott, purchased a large part of the estate in 1857 and built a new imposing mansion called Knowle Hill Park which, in the early years of the 20th century, became the Schiff Home of Recovery. It was demolished some years ago and the offices of Cargill International now occupy the site.

Other parts of the Fairmile Farm estate were developed for smaller detached residences for the better-off, such as those still found in Fairmile Park Road. These were eagerly sought after by city gentlemen who were able to commute to London at first by the train service from Esher and then, in the 1880s, by using the new Guildford line.

Benfleet Hall and Roddam Spencer Stanhope

One of the first of the new houses to be built on the Fairmile estate was the property once called Sandroyd and now called Benfleet Hall in Green Lane. Architecturally, this is one of Cobham's most important buildings. It was built for the artist Roddam Spencer Stanhope by the architect Philip Webb, whose previous commission had been the famous Red House at Bexley for William Morris. Stanhope had moved to Cobham in the middle years of the 19th century and lived

104 *'My Lady of the Mill', by Roddam Spencer Stanhope. (Private Collection)*

105 *Mrs T. Earle of Woodlands.*

for a while at Norwood Farm. He was associated with the Pre-Raphaelite Brotherhood and had worked with the artist Rossetti and the others on the famous Oxford Union murals. Spencer Stanhope used his new home to entertain other artists, such as Burne Jones with whom he painted in the surrounding countryside. His work *The Mill Pond* or *My Lady of The Mill* clearly shows Cobham Mill. Another visitor to Benfleet Hall was the artist George Frederick Watts, who came here with his young bride, the actress Ellen Terry. Ellen, 'beautiful but bored', let down her mass of golden hair until it swept the drawing room floor, much to the horror of the older ladies present.

Sandroyd was later used as a private school started in 1890 by the Reverend Wellesley-Wesley, vicar of Hatchford. One of his pupils was Prince Charles of Saxe-Coburg-Gotha. In 1905 a new school was built on the present site in Sandy Lane pupils would include Randolph Churchill, Anthony Eden, Prince Peter of Yugoslavia and King Hussein of Jordan. The Cobham School was evacuated to Wiltshire during the Second World War and in 1946 Reed's School moved here from Watford.

Mrs Earle and 'Pot Pouri from a Surrey Garden'

Close to Benfleet Hall stood Woodlands, the home of Mrs Theresa Earle, a prolific writer and keen gardener best known for her books in the series 'Pot Pouri from a Surrey Garden'. Mrs Earle was the aunt of the wife of the architect Edwin Lutyens and both he and the great garden designer Gertrude Jekyll visited Mrs Earle at Woodlands. Another visitor was the author Henry James.

Pyports and the Lushingtons

Pyports, which still stands opposite the parish church, seems to have had more than its fair share of distinguished residents during the 19th century. Occupied by Sir William Hoste and then the Currie family, who made their money in banking and distilling, it was let in the 1860s to George Dines, who worked for Thomas Cubitt, the great builder of the age. In about 1870 Pyports became the home of the Lushington family. Stephen Lushington of Ockham Park had been a High Court judge and had, as a barrister, advised both Queen Caroline and Lady Byron on their matrimonial problems. He had also been involved

106 *Pyports, Cobham. A 19th-century view of the rear of the house.*

with William Wilberforce in the fight to abolish slavery.

Stephen's son Vernon moved to Pyports with his wife and three daughters. Vernon, a lawyer by profession, was a Christian Socialist and member of the Positivist Society which propagated what Vernon called 'the beautiful religion of humanity'. Through his connection with the Positivists Vernon became closely involved with a number of the leading intellectuals and writers of his day, including John Ruskin, George Eliot, Charles Kingsley, Mrs Gaskell, Thomas Hardy, Matthew Arnold, Sir Leslie Stephen and F.D. Maurice, who founded the Working Men's College in London. It was through the Working Men's College that Vernon Lushington came to know Dante Gabriel Rossetti, the artist Vernon first introduced

107 *Vernon Lushington of Pyports.*

to Edward Burne-Jones and with whom Rossetti formed a life-long friendship and working relationship.

Vernon's wife Jane was painted by Rossetti in the year of her marriage, and their daughters' portraits were painted by Holman Hunt and Arthur Hughes. Hunt, perhaps best known for *The Light of the World*, visited the Lushingtons at Cobham and attended the wedding of Katherine Lushington at St Andrew's church. The Lushingtons were also great friends with Sir Leslie Stephen and his wife, and the three Lushington girls grew up with Virginia (later Virginia Woolf) almost a sister. Woolf was later to portray Kitty Lushington as Mrs Dalloway in her novel of that title.

108 *Jane Lushington from the portrait by D.G. Rossetti. (Tate Gallery)*

109 *'The Home Quartet', a painting of Mrs Lushington and her daughters at Pyports by Arthur Hughes. (Private Collection)*

110 *This early 20th-century postcard shows Church Cottage, once the home of William Watts, and St Andrew's church.*

Another of the Lushington girls, Margaret, married Stephen Massingberd of Gunby Hall, Lincolnshire at St Andrew's church in 1895, and a cousin of the bridegroom, the young Ralph Vaughan Williams, played the organ on that occasion. Other known visitors were Matthew Arnold and the philosopher Dr. J.H. Bridges. The novelist George Meredith, who lived firstly near Esher and then at Box Hill, was undoubtedly another visitor to Pyports. Although not that wealthy, the Lushingtons played their part in village life and donated to many of the good causes of the time. Vernon was particularly interested in the new Cobham Village Hall and the local school. The barn at Pyports was used as a rehearsal room for a Cobham orchestra under the leadership of Vernon's youngest daughter, Susan.

Church Cottage and William Watts

Just across the road from Pyports, and adjoining the churchyard, stands a house now called Church Cottage. This building probably stands on the site of the medieval Church House. William Watts, a well-known engraver of topographical views, lived in this house from 1814 until his death, shortly before his 100th birthday, in 1851. Although he lived to the year of the Great Exhibition, Watts could distinctly remember the news of the death of Wolfe at Quebec in 1759 and the accession of George III in 1760. He is buried in the churchyard only a few yards from his home.

111   *Overbye, Church Street, home of Leonard Martin, architect.*

Overbye and Leonard Martin

Another of Church Street's fine old houses is Overbye, which stands just across from the lych gate and dates from about 1700. In the early 19th century, Francis Scobie, a tailor, occupied the house. In 1871 Alfred Wiles, another tailor, was living here. Overbye's most famous resident was the architect Leonard Martin FRIBA who moved here in 1897. Martin studied architecture at the Royal Academy School and at the South Kensington School of Art. It was at the latter that he developed a friendship with fellow student Edwin Lutyens. The Arts and Crafts movement in architecture was to become a major influence in the work of both young men.

Martin was particularly active during the time he was at Cobham. He enlarged Overbye and carried out an extensive restoration of Church Stile House. He also enlarged Pyports. In addition to Overbye, Martin purchased the neighbouring property, now known as St Bridgets, which he partly rebuilt. Further along the street he built the properties now known as Homestead and Beech House. Another of Cobham's historic properties to receive attention from Martin was Cobham Court. He also designed the now demolished St John's church, Reed's School, Mount Cottages in Old Common Road, the former church rooms in Spencer Road, the former Cobham Cottage Hospital and St Matthew's School at Downside.

The Bennetts of Leigh Hill

One of the largest farms in Cobham at this time was Leigh Hill Farm, which had been owned by the Bennett family since the 18th century. When Thomas Bennett died in 1878, his sons Thomas Henry and Theodore Joseph inherited the farm, which then extended almost down to the present High Street and out to the Portsmouth Road. T.H. Bennett later purchased the Cobham Court estate and became a popular Master of Fox Hounds. In 1883 the Bennett brothers decided to sell off a large part of Leigh Hill Farm for speculative development and it was at this time that Anyards Road, Copse Road, Hogshill Lane and Cedar Road were laid out. This was the first development of low-cost housing for the middle classes in Cobham and it drastically changed the appearance of the village.

The Crawters

Alongside Charles Combe of Cobham Park and the Bennett brothers, the other major landowning family in 19th-century Cobham was the Crawters. This family is first heard of in the late 18th century when Thomas Crawter, a land agent from Great Bookham, moved to Church Gate House, opposite St Andrew's church. Crawter drew a number of maps of the Cobham area and during his time here he acquired land at the Tilt, the Fairmile and at Downside. He also acquired the former Randalls Farm on the Old Common and Longboyds in Church Street, which became the family's principal residence.

When Thomas died in 1830 he left the property to his three sons, Thomas junior, Henry and William. Henry became one of the members of the first council of the Royal

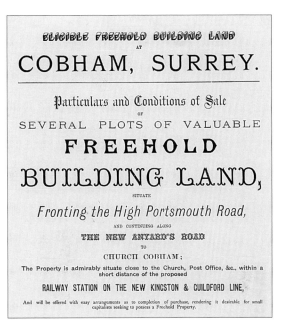

112 *In 1883 the Bennett family sold off part of Leigh Hill Farm for building.*

Institution of Chartered Surveyors and founded the Crawter Prize, which is still awarded to the candidate achieving the highest marks in the Institute's final examination. The Crawter brothers continued to acquire property, including Pyports and Overbye in Church Street and Northfield Farm at Street Cobham. In 1895 most of the family land and houses was sold at a two-day auction, the land described as 'ripe for development' and subsequently built over. In the early part of the following century, the Leg O'Mutton Field was sold off and houses were built on the old road that linked Church Cobham with Street Cobham thereby changing the face of the area forever. Fortunately, plans for housing on the Leg O'Mutton Field did not materialise and it passed to the Esher UDC who have since maintained this surviving portion of the old Church Field as a public open space.

113   *Randalls Farm* c.1914. *The house stood on the edge of the Old Common, opposite the junction of Portsmouth Road and Anyards Road. The site is now occupied by Cobham Gardening Club.*

Cobham in 1861

A wonderful picture of Cobham in the middle of the 19th century has been provided by the somewhat eccentric Arthur J. Munby, barrister, poet and social worker, who visited the village in 1861. It is said that half of Munby's life was spent in cultivated society – he included among his friends Browning, Millais, Rossetti, Swinburne and Ruskin – while the other half was devoted to 'colliery women, fishergirls, milkwomen, female acrobats and the whole sub-world of women manual workers'. The marriage to his maid would have scandalised Victorian society had it not been kept secret from all but a few until after his death. He kept extensive diaries, which include descriptions of the walking tours that he enjoyed so much and provide a unique glimpse into the life of Cobham.

Munby had travelled by train from London to Leatherhead and then walked to Cobham, entering the village from Stoke D'Abernon:

I walked on a mile or more along the flat high road to Cobham Tilt – a few houses on a common – and then just beyond, through Church Cobham, where the village road comes down to the Mole and runs besides it. At the junction stands an old fashioned mill, with a large undershot wheel in full play, and then comes the mill race, a long quiet strip of water broadening out beyond the weir into a pretty view, with old red houses on one side, and willows on the other, and the church spire in the midst.

Few people were about in the village, which is thoroughly rural, and picturesque, though not antique. Seeing 'Cobham Reading Rooms' over the door of a little house, I spoke to the old man who was weeding in the bit of garden in front. The reading rooms flourish, he said, but chiefly through the support of the neighbouring gentry, who established them five years ago. There are three classes of subscribers: the trades people and folk of the better sort are of the first, and these are numerous and take out books to read at home; the labourers don't care to come much and don't take books out. Class 3 is for young men and even boys.

Munby then comes to the real purpose of his visit to Cobham when he meets, seemingly by chance, one of Cobham's working women, the village postwoman. His diary for the previous year reveals that he had spotted her name when she qualified in the Civil Service examinations. In fact, she was the first qualified female letter carrier in the country.

Munby, who had a slightly questionable interest in the appearance of working-class women, especially their hands, seems to have met her in the street and he wrote in his diary: 'I met a tall young woman, who did not seem to belong to any of the ordinary classes of village girls. He face and her hands were sunburnt and weather stained: but her dress was not that of a labouring woman, though it was poor and worn. She had on a battered green velveteen bonnet, a shabby black cloak, and a brown stiff gown of milliner's design.'

Munby then introduced himself and surprised her by announcing that he knew her name – Eliza Harris. Eliza told Munby that she earned 15 shillings a week and walked 18 miles every day except for Sundays when she only walked four or five. Eliza Harris's appointment as a letter carrier in 1860 is confirmed in the Cobham Postmaster's records, as is her dismissal in 1879 for 'detention of letters'.

After visiting Cobham church, Munby took a room at the *White Lion* inn at Street Cobham, from where he provides a wonderful picture of village life:

I came to the White Lion at dusk: had an excellent meal ... in an upper room looking down the broad village street, where groups were lounging in the pleasant idleness that ends the week's work.
After tea, I came down into the bar, where a little group of gossips soon formed. There was the shoemaker, and the builder, and one or two young farmers, and a twinkling old party who had means of his own: and we all sat round and smoked, and talked of the old coaching days, when the White Lion, then twice as big, kept forty horse, and 27 coaches passed to Portsmouth every day, and the shoemaker, who was then an ostler, saved thirty pounds in his first year.
There was talk too of one Richard Dew living near, a jovial man who gives his friends to drink of strong cider and ale, and then chuckles to see them stagger. And of tramps and paupers too: what a number of tickets for food and lodging the Cobham peeler has to give away per night.

Munby then describes the landlady, Jane Rose:

A pleasant nice looking woman of thirty. She and her sister (Mary Jupp) were bustling about, serving many casual customers without, and waiting upon us men with oriental deference. Now and then they would sit a few minutes and join in the talk. The sister said the Cobham people were so stuck up and divided, there was no getting a companion: the tradesmen's daughters thought themselves something, and looked down upon you quite ... In the kitchen close by were the grandparents of the landlady: a fine hale old man of ninety, who had driven over with his coeval wife from Dorking.
So we chatted and smoked till 10.30, when I went up to bed, thinking of that admirable inn-scene in Silas Marner.

114 *Munby's 'old fashioned water mill' in the late 19th century.*

115 *This early photograph of Cobham High Street shows it as it would have looked when A.J. Munby visited in 1860.*

Law and Order

The pace of change in the 18th and 19th centuries, the rising population, high prices during the wars with France and widespread unemployment after, created great hardship for many who based their livelihood on the land, and it seemed that whatever the state of the economy it was they who suffered. In 1810 and 1811 disastrous harvests had driven food prices high and threatened starvation, while the return of the gold standard after 1819 caused falling prices. This hit farmers, who were forced to sack their workers. Added to this, the enclosure of the commons during the preceding century, which had benefited the landowners and yeoman farmers, had detrimental consequences for the cottagers and labourers.

All these events led to a time of great poverty in the 1820s and 1830s. The area most affected was the rural south of England and this resulted in widespread unrest and rioting led by the fictitious 'Captain Swing'. Modern farm equipment, which was reducing the need for manpower, was attacked and destroyed by the rioters, and hayricks were set alight. Landowners received threats to their property and their lives. Many parts of Surrey saw large-scale agitation and soldiers were sent to Dorking and Guildford to quell any trouble there. It seems that even Cobham was not unaffected, a report in the proceedings of a manor court held in 1830 noting, 'a desecration of the Sabbath by the assemblage of disorderly persons in the street opposite the Crown'. The outcome of this event is not recorded but presumably the Cobham landowners were able to placate local people.

The rising local population in the 19th century, together with the spread of new low-cost housing, brought a growing need for improved public amenities. The requirements of local administration were developing far beyond the capacity of the old Vestry system, whose rating powers were limited to the relief of the poor and maintenance of the parish church. Policing continued to be the responsibility of the parish but the unpaid role of parish constable was generally unpopular and sometimes dangerous.

In 1824 the Vestry was fined by the manor court for not having any cage (lock-up) or stocks, and it was agreed to 'build a cage at the south end of the almshouses on the Tilt'. However, this plan was not carried through, and in 1829 it was resolved to build 'a new cage on an octagonal plan with a domed ceiling on the Old Common near the Royal Oak' from plans prepared by Mr Dallen. The office of parish constable disappeared in 1872 and was taken over by the newly formed Surrey Constabulary. The present Cobham police station was eventually opened in the early 1900s.

Church and Chapel

At the end of the 18th century it had been necessary to install galleries in St Andrew's parish church to accommodate the growing congregation. However, the galleries were not enough and in 1825 it was resolved by the Vestry to 'adopt some method to enlarge the church the same not being large enough to admit the inhabitants to attend Divine Service'. The following year a general re-arrangement of the pews was undertaken and a plan in the Vestry book shows the new allocations. A subscription list was drawn up to pay for this work which was headed by HRH Prince Leopold of Claremont, who also

116 *St John's church, Copse Road, photographed shortly before its demolition.*

117 *The former Congregational chapel at Street Cobham.*

owned property in Cobham parish. The sum of £20 was given by the Commissioners of the Navy for a pew allocated 'to the Telegraph' (Chatley semaphore tower). Thomas Page, lord of the manor, was clearly unhappy with these arrangements and he wrote across one whole page of the Vestry Book in 1827 to protest 'against any further alterations or what is called improvement in the interior of the said Church'.

Further alterations followed and in 1853 the south aisle was added. Fortunately the old windows and the Norman door arch were kept and reused. Victorian glass fills the old windows, most of it of average quality, although one addition was the lovely stained glass window over the choir vestry door: its subject is the annunciation and it is from a design by Burne Jones. In 1863 alterations were carried out to the north aisle and it was decided that 'a new chancel arch be built in place of the present one and the Chancel be ornamented'. In 1870 it was 'resolved to light the Church with gas'. Further additions and extensions were made in 1872, 1886 and 1902. It is fortunate that the topographical artist John Hassell visited the church in the 1820s and recorded its appearance prior to these alterations and additions. The organ was presented by Caroline Molesworth of Cobham Lodge in memory of her mother and was installed in 1850 by Messrs J.W. Walker.

In 1899 Miss Carrick Moore of Brook Farm provided the parish with a mission church in Copse Road. The church, dedicated to St John, was designed by the Cobham architect Leonard Martin and contained some important Arts and Crafts fittings and decoration. The building was declared redundant some years ago and regrettably demolished to make way for housing.

The nonconformists continued to flourish in Cobham in the 19th century. Usually they started by meeting in each other's homes before eventually establishing permanent places of worship. In 1818 a room in the house of Daniel Clarke was registered for worship. William Foster, William Dallen and Edward Trigg signed the application. Trigg, a local hairdresser, had been converted under the ministry of a visiting street preacher. A short biography of him, written by a friend shortly after his death, states that he left part of his estate towards the building of a chapel in the village. The evangelist responsible for Trigg's conversion was probably the slightly eccentric Strict Baptist minister, William Huntingdon of Thames Ditton. Huntingdon had become minister of Providence Chapel, Woking in 1776 and later he extended his ministry to nearby villages including Cobham. During his latter years he adopted the style 'William Huntingdon S.S.' (Sinner Saved) and even had this painted on the side of his carriage.

A book on the life of Huntingdon, donated to the former Ebenezer Strict Baptist Chapel in Cedar Road, carries an inscription that the Cobham chapel, 'was one of the many causes founded by William Huntingdon'. This old chapel, now owned by Surrey County Council, was opened for worship in 1873. Another meeting room, registered by the Independents (forerunners of the Con-gregationalists) in 1824, was at the home of Giles Notley. John R. Gayton, an agent of the Surrey Mission who had commenced evangelistic work in Cobham in 1821, signed the application. Notley was the landlord of the *George Inn* at Street Cobham. The Independents are next heard of in 1847 when Miss Mellor of Downside, concerned at the spiritual state of the neighbourhood and what she called 'the sports and heathenish pastimes' that took place on Downside Common on Sundays, opened her home for services. There was considerable disturbance at the first meeting in 1848 when some local youngsters got into the room and let off fireworks. The clubroom at the *George Inn* continued to be used as a temporary place of worship until a chapel was built in 1854 on the site now occupied by Alsford's timber yard. This chapel remained in use until the early part of the last century when it was closed down and demolished. A new Congregational church (now the United Reformed church) was later opened in Stoke Road.

Samuel Bradnack and the Great Revival

Methodism came to Cobham in the 1850s when Samuel Wesley Bradnack and his wife Juliana moved to The Cedars (now Pyports) in Church Street. Samuel was the son of a well-known Wesleyan missionary, Isaac Bradnack, and came to Cobham from Ipswich where he ran a private boarding school. The school moved with him to Cobham and he advertised for pupils in the *Methodist Recorder*, the fees being 60 guineas per annum. A visiting nonconformist minister at this time described Cobham as 'drenched in drink and wickedness'. He considered the village to be 'as dark as heathendom itself' and that 'the teaching of the clergy is cold and semi papistical'. Prompted by the low spiritual state of the village, Bradnack hired a cottage in

118 & 119 *Samuel Wesley Bradnack (left), founder of Methodism in Cobham; and Cobham's first Methodist chapel (right) in Cedar Road shortly before demolition in the 1960s.*

Downside to reach what he called 'the baptised heathens' of the district. His congregation grew and he opened up his home at Pyports for meetings. Eventually the old barn at Pyports was fitted out as a place of worship and students from nearby Richmond Theological College came to preach there. One of the great Methodist divines of the 19th century, Thomas Jackson, also came to preach in the barn.

This was the time of the great 1859 evangelical revival, which spread from the USA to Ulster and then across to England, producing notable Christians like Dr Barnardo, James Chalmers and Hugh Price Hughes. One observer of the Ulster revival was Benjamin Scott of Weybridge, and he seems to have been the man who sparked the religion in Cobham. There are stirring accounts in contemporary religious publications of the meetings in the Pyports barn, of changed lives and of drunkards finding

peace with God. The movement spread from Cobham and preaching centres were set up in Ripley, Ockham, Oxshott, Horsley and other nearby villages. However, as revival spread, so did opposition, particularly from the established church, which eventually forced Bradnack to leave first his home at Pyports and then Cobham. In 1862 the local schoolmaster had burned a copy of the Wesleyan catechism before the whole school to show his contempt for the movement, and a certain 'good woman', on telling the vicar that she now followed the Methodists, was told, 'Then they will lead you to the Devil. The doctrine of assurance is a doctrine of devils'.

From The Cedars, Bradnack moved to another house in Church Street and then to a cottage in the High Street that was used as a chapel. Eventually land for a chapel was purchased in Cedar Road and the building opened in April 1862. For a short period the

120 *Holly Lodge, High Street from an early 20th-century photograph. This was the home of one of Cobham's first Roman Catholic priests who can be seen here with his dog.*

Methodists held meetings in a tent on land near Pyports, and here they witnessed 'a remarkable outpouring of the Holy Spirit'. Bradnack, his family and school eventually moved to Surbiton and then to Folkestone. One of the pupils at Surbiton was Thomas Ansty Guthrie, who later became a well-known writer. His novel *Vice Versa* parodied life at the school and Bradnack was caricatured as the formidable 'Dr Grimstone'. The original Methodist church in Cedar Road was demolished in 1966 and the former Sunday School building was converted into a new church.

Cobham's Roman Catholics

Members of the Roman Catholic Church met in various homes in Cobham during the 19th century, and in 1912 Holly Lodge in the High Street became the home of Cobham's first resident priest. In 1915 Spencer House (now Ham Manor) was acquired in the hope it would become a home for an order of Brigittine priest. Roman Catholics continued to meet in an outbuilding of Ham Manor and in a room at the former *Royal Oak* public house on the Portsmouth Road. In 1930 a temporary church was built in Cedar Road. The present Roman Catholic church was built in Between Streets to the designs of H.S. Goodhart-Rendel in 1957 and is one of the most attractive of all Cobham's more recent buildings.

Private Philanthropy and Public Services

From the middle of the 19th century, successive Acts of Parliament created a welter of District Boards with rate-raising power for particular projects such as roads, drains, schools, street lighting and burials. Local landowners often dominated the Board and a thoughtful, benevolent squire such as Charles Combe would mean a well-cared-for community.

121   *Cobham's first purpose-built school on the Tilt, from a late 19th-century photograph. The building on the left later became the fire station.*

122   *Cobham's first fire engine.*

As in most other villages, schooling in Cobham had been largely a charitable affair. However, in 1833 the Vestry built a National School on land at the Lower Tilt. This building later became a parish room, and soup kitchen, before being converted into the village fire station. As has already been mentioned, Miss Combe built the parochial schools in Cedar Road and an infants' school was later built in Hogshill Lane.

Provision of a local fire engine became a matter of public concern in 1890 following a serious fire at Cobham Court. A letter to the *Surrey Advertiser* revealed that Cobham had 'once possessed a fire engine that had been allowed to rot unused in a field'. It was not until 1898, however, after a further serious fire in the village, that Charles Combe offered to provide the village with a new fire engine that would cost him £500. The Merryweather engine was handed over at a grand ceremony in Cobham Park in 1899. Mrs Combe christened the fire engine and nine visiting fire brigades joined in a spectacular display, throwing jets of water into the lake while the Cobham Brass Band played. The engine was soon put to good use in dealing with fires at Stoke D'Abernon and Cobham Court.

Charles Combe played a key role in providing many of Cobham's public services. Towards the end of the 19th century the burial ground at St Andrew's church was fast filling up, and in 1885 he gave some land on the Tilt to the Cobham Burial Board for the present cemetery. In 1866 Combe organised a public meeting to discuss the desirability of bringing the mains of the Leatherhead Water Company into Cobham and, two years later, he chaired a public

meeting to consider 'the propriety of introducing gas into the parish'. The Cobham Gas Light & Coke Company was formed shortly afterwards with its premises near Cobham Bridge on the site now occupied by Sainsbury's. Street lighting was introduced in 1899 and mains drainage followed a few years after that.

The Poor and the Sick

Health and social welfare went hand-in-hand with the town's development but were, originally, largely matters of local charity backed up by parish support. A Sanitary Committee had been established in 1873 consisting of a number of the leading Cobham residents and the following year it was empowered to spend not more than £50 'to take steps for the repression of scarlet fever in the parish'.

In 1834 the New Poor Law Act provided for the creation of Poor Law Unions to replace local parish units and the Cobham Vestry resolved that it would be most advantageous to be linked with Epsom Union. Cobham's poor were transferred to Epsom Workhouse and the parish workhouse on the Tilt and the parish cottages were sold to Henry Worsfold, the last workhouse master.

One result of the Poor Law Act was the fostering of self-dependence that was manifest in increased membership of the local Friendly Societies. In 1811, the United Brothers Amicable Society was meeting in *The Plough* at Downside, and in 1838 the United Tradesmen met at the *Crown Inn* in the High Street. Towards the end of the 19th century it was the practice of Friendly Societies to join together for a parade around

123   *This view of Cobham High Street* c.*1900 shows either drainage or water pipes being laid.*

Cobham, stopping off at various pubs on the way, and then attend a service in the parish church. In 1890 the Foresters Friendly Society held its thirtieth annual festival at the *White Lion*. In the evening a fête was held in the meadow behind the inn to which 'all the youth and beauty of the village flocked' to be entertained by 'Manley's steam round-about, swings, shooting galleries … and athletic sports. The proceedings were fitly crowned by dancing on the green to the strains of the Cobham band'.

Together with local charitable institutions such as a Coal and Clothing Club, the Friendly Societies enabled many of the poorer people to receive some sort of medical attention. A

parish nurse was later provided and supported by voluntary subscriptions and a 'Cobham Nurse Fund & Home' was led by the Dowager Countess of Ellesmere. A Nurses' Home was built on the Portsmouth Road and the former Cottage Hospital, built in 1905, was opened by HRH The Duchess of Albany, who then lived at Claremont. Voluntary medical assistance was also provided by the St John Ambulance Brigade, formed in 1906, following a series of lectures at Downside by Dr J. Kitchin. Through the assistance of Sir Henry Samuelson of Hatchford Park, a hand-wheeled basket ambulance was acquired for use at the hospital.

124 *A procession of Cobham Friendly Societies passes Leigh Place in the early years of the 20th century.*

125 *HRH The Duchess of Albany opens Cobham's first Cottage Hospital.*

126 *Cobham Cottage Hospital c.1910.*

St Luke's Hostel

Another source of public philanthropy was provided by Miss Shirley Ann Blunt, a lady of independent means who came to live at Church Stile House in 1882. At Church Stile House and at Overbye, across the way, she established St Luke's Hostel, a home both for young women who needed to learn a trade and, later, for elderly gentlewomen. When Miss Blunt died in 1900, the Parish Magazine stated that she had been connected with Cobham for more than twenty years and that in 1883 'she had started her well known home in memory of her beloved friend Miss Armitage'.

127   *Cobham Coffee House and Reading Room in the late 19th century.*

128   *Cobham's first Village Hall in Anyards Road, from an early 20th-century postcard.*

Cobham Library and Village Hall

Better schooling resulted in an increase in literacy and a Reading Room was opened in a house in the High Street in the 1850s. In 1886 another public benefactress, the Countess of Ellesmere, leased the building that is now called 'Envy', at 51 High Street, and opened it as a Coffee House and Reading Room. This was succeeded by a Parish Library that was opened in a house in Cedar Road in 1886. The library later moved to the old Village Hall built by public subscription in 1881 on land in Anyards Road provided by Thomas Bennett of Cobham Court. The new hall was built by Alexander Newland, the local builder.

Howard Paul, a noted American actor and playwright who was very popular in the music halls, supervised the opening concert of the Village Hall, which soon became the centre of much of the local community's activities. The Lushington sisters from Pyports gave a number of concerts in which they invited family friends to take part. Guy Du Maurier, uncle of Daphne Du Maurier, was one who trod the boards at the hall. It is also possible that Ralph Vaughan Williams, a cousin by marriage to the Lushingtons, may have performed at the hall in his youth. In 1889 the newly formed Cobham Brass Band 'discoursed sweet music from the vestibule' of the hall. The band had originally been installed in the gallery but 'their instruments having been chosen for their carrying effect in the open air, proved rather overpowering to sensitive ears'.

Other uses for the hall included religious and political meetings and hunt balls. Many of the new inventions of the day, such as Edison's phonograph and 'the new X rays',

129 *A postcard view of c.1905 showing the* Fox and Hounds, *which stood on the corner of Church Street and High Street. On the right is the* Crown.

were demonstrated here to the amazement of the people of Cobham. In 1894 the inaugural meeting of the new Cobham Parish Council was held in the Village Hall. The creation of various district boards and numerous charitable and voluntary organisations over the years eventually produced a chaos of overlapping authorities, all acting independently of each other. To simplify the system, County Councils were established in 1888 and District Councils in 1895 to deal with matters of local concern. Cobham was initially in the Epsom Rural District but in 1933 it was annexed to Esher Urban District.

Cobham's Brewery and Public Houses

In the 18th century Cobham had been described as 'well furnished with inns'. By the 1850s, the alehouses and inns of Cobham numbered about fifteen and gave the village a certain reputation: 'Drenched in drink and wickedness' was how one visiting non-conformist clergyman described Cobham in 1861. The fact that the village's major source of employment at this time was a flourishing brewery did nothing to help the situation. Cobham's brewery seems to have grown out of premises owned by John Louis Mackay which, in 1803, had been described as 'All that Cottage or Tenement ... known by the name of Homes Place with the Malthouse Brewhouse Yard and Garden thereunto belonging'. These buildings stood on the Portsmouth Road, close to the *White Lion*, on the site now occupied by the Wyndham Court office block, opposite Cobham police station.

In 1806 Mackay sold the brewery to Joseph Stedman of Cedar House and it was he who established the business on a firm footing. On Stedman's death the business passed to his daughter and then to her son, Richard Wallis Ashby, and became known as 'Ashby's Cobham Brewery'. Ashby was much respected in Cobham and was both 'a good churchman and good sportsman'. According to his obituary he also did 'excellent work in the schools' and helped arrange the gas supply.

Most of Cobham's pubs were at some time either owned or controlled by Ashby, the only exceptions being the *Tartar* and the *White Lion*. Many of them have long since disappeared and are remembered in name only. One was the *Crown*, that stood in the High Street on the site now occupied by Threshold Records. Opposite, on the corner of Church Street, stood the *Fox and Hounds*, at one time managed by Henry Glanville, son of John Glanville who kept the *Crown*. The *Fox* was probably the successor to an older inn called the *White Hart* that stood on the opposite corner of Church Street.

Other pubs were the *Swan*, which stood on the Portsmouth Road and seems to have been pulled down in the 18th century; the *Waggon and Horses* on the Downside Road, which later became part of Cobham Stud; the *Royal Oak*, near the corner of Anyards Road and Portsmouth Road; the *King's Arms* near Cobham Bridge, and the *Antelope* which replaced the *George Inn* after it was destroyed by fire in 1865.

130   *The* Little White Lion *from an early 20th-century postcard.*

131 *Cricket on the Tilt in the early years of the last century.*

The *Old Bear* on River Hill was another Cobham Brewery pub, as was the *Harrow* at Downside. In 1881 Cobham Brewery also owned the *Little White Lion* (which had been built by Jeremiah Freeland in the 1720s, the *Running Mare* on the Tilt and the *Old Plough* at Stoke D'Abernon. In 1913 it became the Cobham United Breweries Ltd and eventually closed down in 1922. The premises were purchased by Watney Combe Reid & Co., who used them as a store and off-licence. The last of the brewery buildings was demolished in the 1970s.

Sport and Leisure

Outside the alehouse, recreation could also be found in rural pursuits, and the proximity of the River Mole meant that fishing was a very popular pastime. In the 18th century it was reported that every man in Cobham used to fish and that people even came from London with nets. In the early 19th century,

the lord of the manor erected an eel weir across the river and in 1840 it was reported that 'there is some good angling for pike and perch between Painshill and Esher Place; occasionally a few trout may be taken with the fly, but they are gradually disappearing, the natural result of the all-destroying pike.' The surrounding countryside provided opportunities for hunting and both the stag and the fox remained a popular pursuit for centuries. When the French royal family lived in exile at nearby Claremont, deer were specially carted into the neighbourhood for them to pursue. The local hunt was the Surrey Union, which had its kennels at Cobham Court in 1902. Thomas Henry Bennett of Cobham Court was Master of Fox Hounds for many years.

Cricket, which had been played on the Tilt in the late 18th century, became even more popular in the closing years of the 19th, when a local man and Surrey player, Fred

132   *Cobham Cricket Club in the 1890s. (Surrey History Service)*

133   *Cobham and Downside Rifle Club in the late 19th century.*

Stedman, would often bring the county team down to play the home team. Local enthusiasm for the Tilt Club was demonstrated by the offer of Roland Weller, proprietor of the adjacent carriage works, to give £5 and a bottle of whisky to the first player to hit a boundary through his bedroom window. The Cobham United Cricket Club was formed in the 1880s and had its ground first at Pyports Field and then on the White Lion Meadow. In 1887 it was decided to build a pavilion 'at a not greater cost than £15 and to engage a man for three months to look after the grounds etc at 20s. per week'. The

Tilt Club eventually petered out mostly because of increasing traffic on the Stoke Road and the likelihood of boundary accidents.

Football teams such as the Cobham Hawks were playing regular matches in the late 19th century. In 1886 a football club was formed in connection with the local Coffee Tavern and the vicar offered to supply it with a football. The present Cobham Football Club has its grounds on the Leg O'Mutton Field. A local swimming club existed for some years, making use of the River Mole. Changing rooms were constructed on the banks of the river near the Tilt.

One of the ancient privileges of the manor of Cobham was that of holding a fair on the feast of St Andrew, patron saint of the parish church. The fair was for cows, steers, horses, sheep, and pigs and was held until about 1859 in a field at Street Cobham, on the site now occupied by the house called Faircroft. In 1796 a meadow near Downside Bridge was known as Fair Meadow and was possibly the site of an earlier fair.

For many years the Tilt Green was used for May Day celebrations and a maypole was erected there during the last century. It seems that the very success of the fairs proved to be their downfall. Gypsies and fair people descended on the Green with 'vans of all sorts and kinds of shows, these large steam merry-go-rounds, etc … They brought about 70 horses; were a great annoyance to those living nearby, besides about a dozen wretched donkeys, quite new last year.' Sufficient local opposition gathered for official posters to be printed saying that no more fairs were to be held on the common and the last was held in 1902.

134 *Early motoring in Cobham on the Portsmouth Road near the* Royal Oak.

Road and Rail

In 1836, when the coaching trade was at its peak, some twenty different coaches, including the Royal Mail, passed through Cobham. They carried such romantic and evocative names as *The Star of Brunswick, The Royal Sussex, The Red Rover, The Rocket* and *The Royal Blue.* However, the advent of the railway soon sounded the death knell for this form of transport. In 1844 James Thorne, in his *Rambles By Rivers*, wrote: 'Cobham Street – a pace that prior to the opening of the South-Western Railway had a lively bustling appearance, very different from that which it now wears.'

The invention of the internal combustion engine brought about a reversal in fortunes. One of the first motor cars seen in Cobham was reported by the vicar in the Parish Magazine in 1897:

What at first seemed a very ugly bicycle, but which we soon made out to be a small vehicle on four wheels, containing two people seated one in front of the other. A strong and disagreeable smell of petroleum oil at once revealed that we were watching one of the most recent inventions of this go-ahead age. The car was flying along at the rate of about twelve miles an hour, and we were much struck with the remarkable manner in which it was turned round for a retracing of the way, when the occupants discovered at the Tilt that they had taken the wrong direction. The roads were very dirty at the time and both car and riders were splashed all over with mud. We agree with the many who think that it will be a distant future before these motor carriages become at all popular.

The editor of an earlier *Parish Magazine* had referred to a problem that seems more synonymous with the present century, the damage to buildings caused by 'the practice of driving heavy agricultural engines through the streets at high speed'.

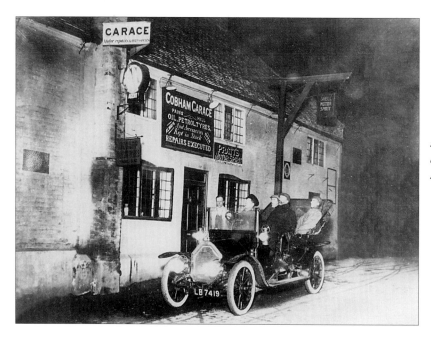

135   *Cobham Motor Works in the early years of the last century. This is now the site of Sainsbury's petrol station.*

His report continued:

> It is no secret that the ancient and picturesque buildings of Church Cobham are beginning to suffer from the finger of time, and the neglect of being dignified by the name of landlords. If to these is added the destructive forces of the demon engine, Church Cobham will be laid in rues long before its time. When these heavy traction engines rush past the whole building trembles from garret to cellar – and recently the new pipes laid by the water company were found to be fractured. If these peripatetic earthquakes are allowed to continue their Mazeppa-like career unmolested, very serious injury to buildings will inevitably ensue.

One of the first garages on the Portsmouth Road was at the former *King's Arms* public house at Street Cobham. The Cobham Garage later became the Cobham Motor Works and was eventually demolished in the 1960s. Its site is now occupied by Sainsbury's petrol station.

Although the first AA cyclist patrols covered the London to Brighton Road, it was not long before these were extended to the Portsmouth Road. The Surrey police were particularly active in setting up speed traps on the road between Kingston and Petersfield, and the stretch between Cobham and Esher including the Fairmile was the most notorious. This section of the road is particularly famous in AA annals because of the prosecution of a patrolman accused of obstructing the police while warning motorists of the existence of a speed trap. He was later arrested on a charge of perjury. Fortunately he was acquitted, but the 'Fairmile Case', as it became known, was one of the first of many occasions when the AA and its patrols appeared in the dock. One prosecution led to the welcome AA salute to members, indicating that the road was free of police speed traps.

The appearance of motor cars on the Portsmouth Road coincided with a famous era in cycling. On another visit to Cobham, A.J. Munby observed, 'Many bicyclists en route: about 12 young women among them, of whom 3 wore breeches and rode astride,' a mode of dress considered rather daring at the time. The Ripley Road, as it became know to cyclists, became a popular run for visitors from London and local tradesmen were quick to take advantage by supplying rest and refreshment as well as cycle repairs. Cobham had at least one cycling club of its own. The landlord of the *White Lion* was 'Bath Road' Smith, a famous cyclist and member of the Bath Road Cycling Club that often used the Ripley Road for excursions. Cobham's Fairmile became the venue for cycle racing as early as 1870.

Carriers plied their trade on the local roads, delivering goods from one village to the next, and the local omnibus ran from Ripley to Esher Station in 1870 to meet the London train. When Arthur Munby came to Cobham the nearest railway station was at Leatherhead, but only a few years later there were a number of abortive attempts to bring the railway into Cobham. Only one of the proposed schemes got as far as an inquiry at the House of Lords and this was supported by several prominent local residents including Charles Combe of Cobham Park and William Worsfold of Ham Manor, who both voiced their hopes that it would bring an increase in both trade and development to the area. Combe was anxious to provide his estate at Cobham Park with coal, which was at that time brought by barge to Thames Ditton and then carted to Cobham. The line would also

136 *C.A. 'Bath Road' Smith, standing third from the left, landlord of the* White Lion *and pioneer cyclist, with other members of the Bath Road Cycling Club at Cobham in 1896.*

137   *Cobham railway station in the early years of the 20th century.*

assist him in transporting farm produce to markets at Kingston and London.

Not all Cobham residents were in favour of the scheme and John Earley Cook of Knowle Hill expressed a personal concern that his coach and four (one of the few in the district) would not be able to negotiate the proposed level crossing at Fairmile Lane. He was also concerned about the inevitable and what he considered detrimental increase in the population. The proceedings of the inquiry offer no reason why the scheme was not adopted, but the *Surrey Advertiser* referred to a note in the Court Circular which stated that Sir Thomas Biddulph intended to oppose the scheme on behalf of HM Queen Victoria, who considered that the proposed new line would pass too close to her much loved home

at nearby Claremont, and would be an intrusion into her privacy.

The present railway station on the Waterloo-Guildford line was eventually opened on 2 February 1885. In its first year the journey to London took 51 minutes. The first local railway accident appears to have taken place ten years later, when Joseph Robbins of Paddington was knocked down and his 'fearfully mutilated body' found near the station.

Postal Services

Before the opening of the Guildford line, the mail was taken to Weybridge and then carted to Cobham, the post office being at Street Cobham. When Cobham station was opened the post office moved to a new

138 *Cobham Post Office c.1905.*

building in the High Street which is now the Royal Mail sorting office. The postmaster, George Samuel White, a somewhat formidable character, erected this building and the strict disciplinarian regime is borne out by entries in his Day Book.

Private Enterprise

The county directories of the 19th century provide a clear picture of the various trades, industries, and shops that were required to service the growing community. These still tended to cater chiefly for local needs and there was little manufacture on a large scale, save for brewing and milling.

Cobham Mill was enlarged by the building of the present mill in the 1820s. However, one of the millers, Daniel Dallen, saw the need to move with the times and built a large steam-driven mill in Hollyhedge Road, at the rear of the present Barclays Bank. Dallen prospered from his enterprises and built Holly Lodge in the centre of the High Street as a home for himself and his family. This elegant and much loved building formed an imposing centrepiece for the High Street. It was later used as the showrooms for the South Eastern Gas Board but was demolished in the 1960s to make way for a nondescript parade of shops.

In 1871 Mrs Batchelor was the 'Master Miller employing five men and one boy' at Cobham Mill. Her nephew Thomas Sweetlove took a lease of the mill in 1890. Henry Moore and Son later purchased it and Mrs Earle, in *A Third Pot-Pouri from a Surrey*

139   *Pile driving at Cobham Mill in the early years of the last century.*

Garden, commended them for their various flours and fresh bran. A tragedy occurred at the mill in the early years of the 20th century when Harold Lynn, who the *Parish Magazine*

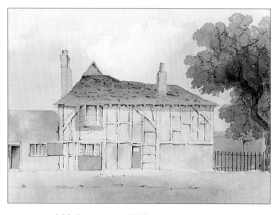

140   *Old houses in Cobham High Street from a watercolour painted in 1827 by Edward Hassell. These buildings were replaced by Gammon's Store in 1897. This is now the site of Cobham Furniture. (British Library)*

described as 'one of the most deservedly popular and promising young men of the village', was accidentally killed while assisting workmen to repair the wheels. The mill was sold to Charles Harvey Combe in 1925 and was threatened with demolition. However, in 1926 the *Surrey Comet* confidently stated that 'there is no danger, we understand, of the old mill either being destroyed or becoming altogether derelict. The reason for the present stoppage is that Messrs H. Moore and Son, who have been millers there for many years, are not renewing the lease.' The mill survived until 1953, when the older portion that jutted out into the road was demolished. The mill is now held by the Cobham Mill Preservation Trust, who have done a wonderful job of restoring it to full working order.

Alexander Raby's Iron Mills at Downside were dismantled in 1814 and converted for use as a flock or rag mill. It was purchased by Charles Combe of Cobham Park in 1865 and converted for generating electricity for his new mansion.

In the 19th century the High Street consisted of little more than Holden's forge, Foster's dairy, a wheelwright's and a few houses. John Hassell painted two water-colours of the High Street in the 1820s and one of these shows the picturesque timber-framed building that was replaced by Gammons Departmental Store towards the end of the century. Cobham Furniture now occupies the site. At the end of the 19th century and during the early years of the next, a number of purpose-built shops were erected at the other end of the High Street and a new

post office was built on the corner of Hogshill Lane.

For much of the 19th century Church Street was the commercial centre of Cobham, and here could be found a stationer, a butcher, a grocer, a milliner and a seedsman. Eldred Ledger the watchmaker, known locally as 'Tickety', lived and worked in the little 18th-century building which now houses 'Phoenix'. In 1857 George Brown of Chertsey purchased the premises now occupied by 'Envy' and set up business as a saddle and harness maker. In 1859 he was described as 'Sadler and Harness Maker, Stable Furnisher & Rope, Line and Twine Maker'. His business prospered and he purchased adjoining land, on which he built new premises that, until recently, were owned by his descendants and known as 'Brown's Sports Shop'.

141 *This building in Church Street was the home and workplace of Eldred 'Tickety' Ledger, Cobham's watch repairer in the 19th century.*

142   *Brown's shop, High Street, in the late 19th century.*

In 1888 the *Parish Magazine* included advertisements for W. Harding's Livery Stables at the White Lion Hotel Yard – 'Broughams, Landaus and Open Flys always in Readiness'; Joseph Hutchinson – 'Corn, Seed, Flour & Coal Merchant'; James Lynn – 'Family Butcher'; F. Holden – 'Whitesmiths & Smiths Work in all its branches'; C. Souter – 'Fancy Stationer and Newsagent', and T.C. Andrew – 'Cigar and Tobacco Stores, Hair Dresser and Ornamental Hair Worker.'

In the latter part of the 19th century, brick-making became an important local industry and there were two brickfields on the border of Cobham and Oxshott. The smaller one belonged to H.W. Scriven, of Tudor Court in Fairmile Park Road, a strong non-conformist and staunch teetotaller. It occupied some five acres of ground alongside Knipp Hill and was in production for about

40 years, turning out 1,500 hand-made bricks per man-day. Scriven's teetotal principle led him to purchase the *Griffin Inn* that stood at the top of Knipp Hill and close it down. His business closed in 1939, largely due to the shortage of clay and difficulties over labour. The site was purchased and levelled by a Mr Goldsmith and is now occupied by the Pony Chase estate.

The larger of the brickfields belonged to John Earley Cook, who came to Cobham in the 1860s. He purchased the Knowle Hill estate and built the house which until recently formed part of the Schiff Hospital. Cook's brickfield lay next to Littleheath and occupied about thirty acres. Cook was a colourful character; much loved and respected by his employees but considered a rather difficult and obstinate man by others in the community. In 1885 he was elected Master of the Worshipful Company of Carpenters of London. In the middle years of the century he had objected to the plans to bring the railway into the centre of Cobham. However, in 1883 he sold part of his brickyard to the London and South Western Railway, who conveniently provided a siding so that London refuse could be brought down and burned and the ashes used to make a cheaper type of brick. The level crossing in Little Heath Lane is now known as Cook's Crossing. Cook's directorship of the railway had no doubt helped in getting the line to pass through his land.

By all accounts, Cook's 'brickies' and their families were well cared for and received Christmas presents of brandy, poultry and coal. A free medical service was provided, as was the 'iron hut' which became a community centre and was also used as an evening games club for the men and an infants school for the children who were too young to walk to Cobham or Oxshott schools. In the afternoons, the local women met there for a chat, passing their time sewing and knitting, and on Sunday afternoons it was used for church services.

Cook died at Knowle Hill in 1904 aged 81 and was buried in the family vault at Cheshunt. His kindness and generosity were evidenced by his will, in which the sale proceeds of the Knowle Hill estate – up to £30,000 – were left to the Peabody Donation Fund. Other gifts were to hospitals and charitable organisations. Many of the longer-serving employees received annuities of up to £30. Cook's brickyard was later taken over by W.E. Benton, who found the site had considerable drainage problems. Canadian soldiers occupied the site during the two world wars, the brickyard was finally closed in 1960, and modern houses have now been built around the water-filled clay pit.

Matthew Arnold at Cobham

One of the greatest thinkers and writer of 19th-century England, Matthew Arnold, came to live in Cobham in 1873. With his wife and children he moved to Painshill Cottage, part of the Painshill estate. Tragically, the house was demolished in the 1960s and is now the site of Matthew Arnold Close. Despite his unorthodox personal religious beliefs, Arnold and his family were regular attenders at St Andrew's church. While at Cobham he published a number of his most important works including *God and the Bible* and *Last Essays on Church and State*.

Arnold and his family loved Cobham as is shown in a letter which he wrote to a friend:

> The cottage we have got there is called Pains Hill Cottage … The country is beautiful – more beautiful than even the Chilterns, because there is heather and pines, while the trees of other kinds, in the valley of the Mole, where we are, are really quite magnificent. And St George's Hill and wood of I know not how many acres, practically quite open, is a continual pleasure. We are planting and improving about our cottage as if it were our own and we had a hundred years to live there; its great merit is that it must have had one hundred years of life already, and is surrounded by great old trees – not the raw sort of villa one generally has to take if one wants a small house near London.

The cottage was let to Arnold by his friend Charles Leaf, who then owned the Painshill estate. In 1831 it had been described as 'an elegant cottage *ornée*'. There were wonderful views from the house to Painshill with its great cedars and beautiful landscaped park.

143 *Matthew Arnold from the portrait by G.F. Watts.*
(National Portrait Gallery)

144 *Painshill Cottage, home of Matthew Arnold.*

Arnold was often at Painshill House to dine with the Leafs and play billiards. In fact, the family were allowed to use the park as if it were their own. Skating on the frozen lake was a favourite winter pastime. Walking and riding were Arnold's other two great pleasures and he would often walk 'the Burwood round'

with his dogs, through the grounds of his neighbour and friend the Countess of Ellesmere.

Family pets were an important part of the Arnold family life. The death of his pony Lola at Cobham caused him much sadness. Max and Geist were two of 'the dear, dear dogs'. When Geist died in 1880 Arnold wrote the poem 'Geist's Grave', and Kaiser was another dog immortalised in verse. In addition to various cats, another member of the household was his daughter's canary, Matthias. When the bird died in 1882 it, too, became the subject of a poem. Arnold and his wife loved gardening and Matthew Arnold's printed journals contain many references to working in the garden.

The family became thoroughly involved in the life of the local community and subscribed to charities such as the Clothing Club, the Coal Club and the School Trust. Matthew Arnold subscribed to the building of the new village hall and his wife was involved in many of the ladies' organisations of the parish. On at least two occasions Matthew and his wife entertained village mothers and their children to a Christmas tea at the Working Men's Hall which Charles Leaf had provided in Street Cobham. When Lucy Arnold married Frederick Whittridge, a wealthy American, in December 1884, it was the chief event in the Cobham social calendar. Local builders erected arches and other decorations along the route from Painshill Cottage to St Andrew's church. Celebrities came down from London and people stood on the pews better to see and chatter about them, behaviour for which they were afterwards reprimanded by the vicar. The signatures on the marriage register

145 *An election group outside the* Crown Inn *c.1878. On the wall is a poster carrying the slogan 'Vote For Cubitt'. George Cubitt was MP for West Surrey between 1860 and 1884.*

146 *Holden's Forge c.1890. This stood in the middle of the High Street on the site now occupied by Iceland.*

147   *Shooting party on the Hatchford Park estate in the 19th century. Charles Combe of Cobham Park is seen standing second from the right.*

include W.E. Forster, the great educationalist, and Henry James, the author.

Although Arnold once described himself as 'the hermit of the Mole', his life at Cobham was certainly not that of a recluse. Many friends enjoyed the warmth of the family's hospitality, including his niece, the writer Mrs Humphrey Ward, who later recalled 'the modest Cobham cottage … the garden beside the Mole where every bush and flower bed had its history; and that little study-dressing room where some of the best work in nineteenth century letters was done'. In 1885 he received warning signs of the illness that was to lead to his death. He wrote of 'horrid pains across my chest' and realised that, like his father and grandfather, he had angina pectoris. He cut back his outdoor pursuits by giving up tennis and reducing his skating

at Painshill. In a letter he wrote, 'imagine my having to stop half a dozen times in going up Pains Hill!'

In April 1888 Matthew Arnold died of heart failure in Liverpool, where he had travelled to meet his daughter and family returning from America. His body was brought back to Cobham and then taken to be buried near other family graves at Laleham. For many years after his death his study was kept as he had left it and Mrs Humphrey Ward recalled 'his coat hanging behind the door, his slippers beside the chair, the last letters he had received, and all the small and simple equipment of his writing table ready to hand.' Although Arnold and his wife are not buried in Cobham, a small brass plate to their memory was placed in St Andrew's church by the Ellesmere family of Burwood.

Ten

THE TWENTIETH CENTURY

Whether Cobham is now a village or a town is still hotly contested in certain quarters. What is certain is that the 20th century saw Cobham develop from a rural country village with a population of about 4,000 into a thriving community with a population of over 10,000. The size of the original parish of Cobham was drastically reduced in the early years of the 20th century when the north-east portion was taken into the newly created parish of Oxshott. At the same time, a large part of the parish south of the river Mole, including Downside, was taken into Ockham and Hatchford.

Residential and Commercial Development

In the 1890s shops began to appear in what is now the High Street and farmland was given over to housing development in new roads such as Anyards Road, Leigh Road, Freelands Road, Hogshill Lane, Cedar Road and Tilt Road. Other new houses were built along parts of the Portsmouth Road. As the new century progressed so the need for more and more housing grew. Old estates such as that at Brook Farm on the Stoke Road were broken up for development and the Oxshott Way estate was laid out on the former Mizen's Nursery. Some of the larger 19th-

century houses on the Fairmile were pulled down to make way for smaller more convenient properties. The demolition of a house called 'The Garth', Miles Lane, designed by the noted Arts and Crafts architect M.H. Baillie Scott, was a great loss. Fortunately, Philip Webb's 'Benfleet Hall' was saved from demolition after representations to the Housing Minister in the House of Commons.

In the 1930s and '40s further changes occurred with the arrival of council housing on the site of the former Northfield Farm at Street Cobham, opposite which the Savoy Cinema was built. Further residential development took place on the Tartar Fields between the Portsmouth Road and Hogshill Lane. But probably the most significant changes in the appearance of Cobham took place in the 1960s. The local authority had plans to pedestrianise the High Street and construct a by-pass from the Tilt to Downside Bridge and across to the foot of Painshill. Whilst destroying some of the surrounding countryside, the implementation of this plan might well have saved a number of old buildings that were subsequently lost.

After a decision not to implement it, the next plan was to widen the High Street and create a dual carriageway. This was the plan

148 *Cobham High Street in the 1920s.*

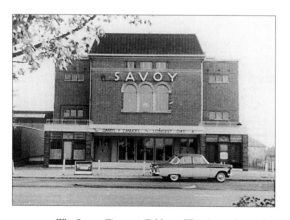

149 *The Savoy Cinema, Cobham. This formerly stood on the Portsmouth Road between the* White Lion *and the Recreation Ground.*

that was accepted and partially implemented. Regrettably, it resulted in the demolition of practically all the old buildings on River Hill together with the *Fox and Hounds* pub and some of the buildings at the entrance to Church Street. The only buildings to survive were the *Old Bear* and La Capanna, and the latter was only saved by the formation of Cobham Conservation Group. The development that replaced the old cottages on River Hill involved little imagination and was described at the time as looking like 'a match box on stilts'.

Further along the High Street, Kippins shop was demolished together with the old United Dairies building and Holly Lodge, all of which were replaced by unimaginative building typical of the 1960s. On the opposite site, Gammons Store, built in 1897, was demolished to make way for the building now housing Cobham Furniture. The original plan was to take the building line back and this would have involved the demolition of the little building now housing 'Envy' and 'Questa'; the Threshold Records building was in fact put on the new building line. But a campaign led by the Cobham Conservation Group persuaded the Council to retain the existing building line. Unfortunately, the building that replaced Gammons was something of an architectural compromise.

At the other end of the High Street, 'Broxmore', a Victorian house that stood in the angle between Anyards Road and Between Streets, was demolished to make way for the double parade of shops called Oakdene Parade. One of the few good buildings from this period is the Roman Catholic Church of the Sacred Heart designed by H.S. Goodhart-Rendel.

Perhaps one of the most important physical changes to the area around Cobham was the construction firstly of the Cobham and Esher by-pass and then the building of the M25 motorway which cut a great swathe through the countryside to the south of Downside.

150   *The top of River Hill during the widening of the road in the 1960s. The only building to survive is La Capanna next to 'Teetgens'. (Compare this with illustration 93 on page 87.)*

151   *Kippins Shop in the High Street shortly before demolition in the 1960s.*

152   *The former United Dairies Building (right) in the High Street c.1960. Dating from about 1900, this building was replaced by the block now housing Matchpoint and Bottoms Up. To the right of this building stood Holly Lodge (see illustration 154).*

153 *Laying the first tarmac surface on Anyards Road, near the junction with Freelands Road. The Tartar Fields can be seen in the distance on the left.*

Conservation in Cobham

The Cobham Conservation Group was formed in 1973 after the Cobham Residents' Association had been instrumental in the creation of the town's first Conservation Area, which took in Church Street and the riverside. Since then three further areas have been created at Downside, Plough Corner and the Tilt. For a long period in the 1930s the local newspaper contained letters concerning the need for a footbridge over the River Mole at Ashford. A bridge was eventually constructed towards the end of the last century and this now links all the conservation areas, thereby providing a very pleasant circular walk around Cobham.

There have been several other success stories in the preservation of Cobham's historic past, probably the most important being the restoration of Cobham Mill. A successful campaign instigated by the Conservation Group and taken up by the Cobham Millers resulted in a full restoration of the building to working condition. Other highlights are the restoration of the semaphore tower on Chatley Heath by Surrey County Council and of the famous landscape park at Painshill.

Commercial Enterprise

Cobham had its first 'chain' store in the late 1890s, when James Fielder Gammon opened his shop in the High Street supplying clothing and drapery. Gammon's opened other stores in Guildford and Woking. In the 1950s Cobham had the first self-service

154   *Cobham had the first self-service Woolworth's in the country. It can be seen here in this 1960s view of the High Street. The large house is Holly Lodge and just across the road can be seen the petrol pumps for the former Soanes Garage.*

Woolworth Stores in the country. Between 1918 and 1932 Fairmile Cottage, on the Portsmouth Road between Cobham and Esher, was the home of Invicta Cars, founded by Noel Macklin. When the business was sold off in 1933 Macklin started a new company called Fairmile Engineering, which imported chassis from the USA onto which it built its own cars. Reid Railton of *Bluebird* and Napier Railton land-speed-record fame became a consultant and lent his name to a new car which became the fastest and most successful of the British Straight-Eights in the 1930s, some 1,400 being produced and sold. 'He shall have chariots faster than air' was the slogan adopted to introduce the Railton, which

Autocar magazine summed up as 'ten years ahead of its time'.

The sales of cars dropped off in the late 1930s and Railton Cars were sold to the American Hudson Motors in 1939. It was decided to concentrate on the war effort, and Fairmile Engineering Company made a fast patrol boat of a type that could be produced in quantity. The 'Fairmile' motor gunboat saw extensive wartime service and earned Macklin a knighthood in 1946. After the war Fairmile Engineering was taken over by the Ministry of Defence. In recognition of the secret work done here the Admiralty presented Cobham with the ship's bell from HMS *Cobham* and this now hangs in the Borough Council's offices.

Visions of the Future

In the 1890s C.A. 'Bath Road' Smith advertised 'acres for aeros' on his meadow behind the *White Lion* inn at Street Cobham. Fortunately, this particular scheme did not prove successful. However, the close proximity of Brooklands at Weybridge, where so many pioneering motor and aviation events took place, brought Cobham close to the centre of the development of modern-day travel.

Flying machines of a different sort were in the mind of writer H.G. Wells. In his book 'War of the Worlds' he writes of a Martian invasion near Woking and places some of the action in Cobham, where a man climbs the spire of St Andrew's church to look out for the approaching invaders.

A Popular Residential Area

In 1919 David Lloyd George made his home at The Firs (now called Upper Court) on the Portsmouth Road between Cobham and Esher. Just across the road from Upper Court stood The Homewood and it was here, in the 1920s, the Infanta Beatrice of Spain, daughter of Alfred, Duke of Edinburgh, and sister-in-law to King Ferdinand of Romania, came to live to be near her sons who were being educated at nearby Sandroyd School. During her time here Beatrice entertained members of her family such as the flamboyant Queen Marie of Romania. Queen Alexandra and her grandson the Prince of Wales were also visitors to The Homewood. The property next to The Homewood, known as Winterdown, was then owned by the Butler family, who also owned Heywood. The property was rented out to Locker Lamson, a rather bizarre and well known Liberal MP. It seems that

155   *David Lloyd George, who made his home at The Firs (now Upper Court) between Cobham and Esher in the early years of the last century. (National Portrait Gallery)*

during his time at the property he arranged for Albert Einstein to visit and that Einstein had a hut built in the surrounding woods where he could play his violin.

Queen Marie of Romania came again to Cobham in 1934. Her eleven-year-old grandson, Prince Peter of Yugoslavia, was at Sandroyd and in October 1934 the young boy was woken from his sleep to be told his father King Alexander had been assassinated and he was now King. Peter's mother was too unwell to come to her son and so the formidable Marie made the journey. The building that Queen Marie knew and wrote of lovingly in her autobiography was demolished in the 1930s and replaced by one of the first 'modernist' houses to be built in the country. This property, designed by Patrick Gwynne and also called The Homewood, is now the property of the National Trust and will eventually be opened to the public.

156   *Sir Thomas Sopwith, pioneer aviator, who lived at Compton House, Fairmile Park Road in the early years of the last century.*

Aviation pioneer Sir Thomas Sopwith lived at Compton House in Fairmile Park Road in Cobham between 1914 and 1920. He sold the house to Philip Lyle, a member of the sugar-refining family.

Entertainment and Scandal

For many years Cobham's first Village Hall in Anyards Road was the centre of village social life. It was here that the first films in Cobham were shown and a lending library set up. In August 1914 the hall 'was packed with Cobham men eager to hear of their country's need and to declare their willingness to render personal service in whatever way their age and opportunities made possible'. Many of those young men were not to return

and their names are now recorded in the war memorial chapel of St Andrew's church.

In 1938, the *Daily Mirror* newspaper carried the headline 'Dance Morals Trial Held Up By Roars of Village'. Cobham Councillor Thomas Daly, a trustee of the hall, had, according to *John Bull* magazine, 'claimed that "the orgies which take place after these hectic hops" rival those of Sodom and Gomorrah, the "disgusting scenes" presented including first aids to nausea as "girls and boys cuddling and kissing in dark corners"'. A public enquiry was held at the Village Hall and the national press had a field day, with headlines such as 'Cobham Village Hall "Orgies" Inquiry'. During the course of the enquiry Daly was accused of being 'a trouble making,

157 *This arch was put across Between Streets to welcome soldiers returning home from the First World War.*

158 *A humorous view of the events at Cobham Village Hall in 1938.*

scandal mongering, publicity loving, dishonest old man.' The proceedings concluded that Daly's statement, 'though he eventually limited his complaint to two occasions, seems to have been made very wildly and without taking reasonable steps to ascertain the facts.' The *Daily Mail* announced 'Surrey's Cobham is no Gomorrah. The Village has been vindicated.'

The excitement quickly died down and the episode was overshadowed by the Second World War, when the hall was put to use as British Restaurant, a gas mask distribution depot, a First Aid Post and an ARP centre.

National Events

Cobham suffered relatively little during the Second World War, although a number of bombs fell in the district as well as several V2 rockets. Vickers Armstrong at nearby Weybridge suffered a particularly devastating air raid, killing many local people. Anti-aircraft guns for the protection of London were stationed at Tartar Hill on an area still known as 'the gun site'. Canadian soldiers were stationed in Cobham during the course of the war and the hospital playing fields near Cobham station were used as an airfield for a while. Cobham did not let the coronation

159 *The residents of Spencer Road celebrate the Coronation in 1953. The author is one of the youngsters enjoying the party.*

160 *Severe flooding at Cobham in 1968 virtually cut off all road communication for 24 hours. This photograph was taken by the author outside the Cobham Motor Works at the foot of Painshill. This is now the site of Sainsbury's petrol station.*

of our present Queen go unmarked, and street parties were one popular way of celebrating the great day.

In 1968 Cobham was hit by one of the worst floods in at least a century. The River Mole flooded the road at the foot of Painshill. The railway track near Cobham station was washed away in parts and water flowed between the two platforms. A large piece of the centre section of Downside Bridge collapsed and Cobham was virtually cut off for 24 hours. Following the Great Storm of 1987, fallen trees closed many local roads.

Cobham in the Headlines

Twice in the last century Cobham made the headlines in the national press. The first time

was when a young woman from Leigh Road was shot down and killed by her husband on Oakdene Parade in 1967. Two years earlier a local man, Frank Clifton Bossard of Lodge Close, Stoke D'Abernon, was caught spying for the Russians in 1965. Local residents were shocked to find that their apparently respectable neighbour had been involved in selling secrets to the Soviets. Bossard was instructed by his Russian employers to leave messages in what were called 'dead letter boxes' dotted around the local countryside. He was once told to meet a Soviet agent outside Cobham railway station who was to give a password that was something like: 'Didn't I meet you in a French village?' The correct answer was, 'No, in 1961 I was in

161   *A coin of Magnentius (A.D. 350-353) from the Chatley Farm Roman bath house site found during a fieldwalking survey iundertaken in September 2003. (see page 7) By permission of Giles Pattison and Surrey County Archaeological Unit.*

Lisbon.' Although the whole episode now sounds like something from a Le Carré novel, it was a great shock to the security services of the time.

'Constant change is here to stay'

Increasing population has brought more houses – sometimes at the cost of older buildings. Facilities provided by Victorian philanthropy became outdated and were taken over by the local authority. New buildings replaced the Cottage Hospital on Tartar Hill and the schools in Cedar Road, a new secondary school being opened in Lockhart Road in 1958. Thirty years later, when secondary education was moved out of Cobham, this became St Andrew's First and Middle School, and the Cedar Road buildings were converted into library and adult education facilities.

Housing has been provided for the elderly together with a thriving Day Centre, and, close by, a new Village Hall has replaced the building that once stood in Anyards Road. Unfortunately, some new additions have failed to make any valuable architectural addition to Cobham, as is the case with the modern telephone exchange insensitively placed in Church Street, the development of River Hill and some of the new shops in the High Street. As a new century is entered, with all the pressures this will bring, the people of Cobham should remain vigilant. A healthy respect for the past will be needed when planning for the future of a community that is now over two thousand years old.

SELECT BIBLIOGRAPHY
AND FURTHER READING

Albert, W., *The Turnpike Road System in England 1663-1840* C.U.P. (1972)

Allison, W., *My Kingdom For A Horse* Grant Richards (1919)

Arnold, M., *Letters 1848-1888* (2 vols., Macmillan & Co. (1895)

Aubrey, John, *History of Surrey (1718-19)* Kohler & Coombes (1975)

Bailey, M., *The English Manor* Manchester U.P. (2002)

Bassett, S. (ed.), *The Origins of Anglo-Saxon Kingdoms* Leicester Univ. Press (1989)

Bates, A., *Virginia Woolf – A Biography* The Hogarth Press (1972)

Bennett, H.S., *Life on the English Manor* Cambridge (1937)

Bird, J. & D.G. (ed.), *The Archaeology of Surrey to 1540* Surrey Archaeological Society (1987)

Blair, J., *Early Medieval Surrey – Landholding, Church and Settlement* Alan Sutton & Surrey Arch. Soc. (1991)

Bradstock, A. (ed.), *Winstanley and the Diggers 1649-1999* Frank Cass (2000)

Brandon, P., *A History of Surrey* Phillimore & Co. (1977)

Brayley, W.E., *History of Surrey* (1850 and later)

Brockway, Fenner, *Britain's First Socialists* Quartet (1980)

Cam, H.M., *The Hundred and the Hundred Rolls* Merlin Press (1963)

Campbell, M., *The English Yeoman Under Elizabeth and the Early Stuarts* The Merlin Press (1942)

Chambers, R., *The Strict Baptist Chapels of England: Surrey & Hants*

Cleal, E.E., *The Story of Congregationalism in Surrey* (1908)

Colvin, H., *A Biographical Dictionary of British Architects 1600 – 1840* Yale Univ. Press (1995)

Copeland, J., *Roads and their Traffic 1750-1850* David & Charles (1968)

Crocker, G. (ed.), *Alexander Raby, Ironmaster* Surrey Industrial History Group (2002)

Crooks, Rev. F.W., *The Parish Church of St. Andrew, Cobham* (1960)

Defoe, D., *A Tour Through The Whole Island of Great Britain* (1724 & 1742)

Dictionary of National Biography

Dyer, C., *Everyday Life in Medieval England* Hambledon & London (1994)

Dyer, C., *Making a Living in the Middle Ages* Penguin (2003)

Earle, Mrs T., *Pot-Pourri from a Surrey Garden, More Pot-Pourri from a Surrey Garden, A Third Pot-Pourri* Smith Elder and Co. (1899-1903)

Earle, Mrs T. and Miss E. Case, *Pot-Pourri Mixed By Two* Smith Elder and Co. (1914)

Edwards, P., *Rural Life – A Guide to Local Records* Batsford (1993)

Fairfax Lucy, A., *The Lucys of Charlecote*

Gaunt, W., *The Pre-Raphaelite Tragedy* Sphere Books (1975)

Gelling, M., *Place-Names in the Landscape* J.M. Dent and Sons (1984)

Greenwood, G., *Elmbridge Water Mills* (1980)

Hadfield, M., *A History of British Gardening* John Murray (1960)

Harris, R., *Discovering Timber-Framed Buildings* Shire (1978)

Haynes, R., *Esher Quakers* (1971)

Hill, C., *The World Turned Upside Down* Penguin (1975)

Hill, C. (ed.), *Winstanley - The Law of Freedom and Other Writings* Pelican Classics (1973)

Hillier, J., *Old Surrey Watermills* Skeffington and Son Ltd (1951)

Horne, P., *The Rural World 1780-1850* Hutchinson (1980)

Horne, P., *Labouring Life in the Victorian Countryside* Alan Sutton (1987)

Hoskins, W.G., *The Making of the English Landscape* Hodder and Stoughton (1955)

Hudson, D., *Munby – Man of Two Worlds* John Murray (1972)

Hunt, R. (ed.), *Hidden Depths – An Archaeological Exploration of Surrey's Past* Surrey Arch. Soc. (2002)

Huntingdon, W., *The Bank of Faith* (Centenary Edition) (1913)

Janes, H., *The Red Barrel – A History of Watney Mann* John Murray (1963)

Jewell, H.M., *English Local Administration in the Middle Ages* David & Charles (1972)

Kitz, N. & B., *Pains Hill Park* Norman Kitz (1984)

Knight, C., *Caroline Bauer and the Coburgs* (1887)

Langham-Carter, R.R., *Painshill Cottage – Matthew Arnold's Surrey Home* Surrey Arch. Soc. Collections Vol. 67; *The Arnolds at Painshill Cottage* Surrey Arch. Soc. Collections Vol. 69

Lennard, R., *Rural England* Oxford (1959)

Linden, J. (ed.), *Alfieri Revisited* Supplement to *The Italianist* No. 21 (2001)

Malcolm, J., *Modern Husbandry of Surrey* (1804-1814)

Manning, O., & Bray, W., *The History and Antiquities of the County of Surrey* (1804-14)

Mason, R.T., *Timber-Framed Buildings of England* Coach Publishing

Millward R. & Robinson D., *Landscapes of Britain Series: Thames and the Weald* Macmillan

Molesworth, C., *The Cobham Journals* Edward Stanford (1880)

Moorman, M., *William Wordsworth* Oxford

Morris, J. (ed.), *History from the Sources: Domesday Book: Surrey* Phillimore 1975

Nairn, I. & Pevsner, N., *The Buildings of England – Surrey* Penguin (1971)

Orr, J.E., *The Second Evangelical Awakening in Britain* Marshall Morgan & Scott (1949)

Pocock, W.W., *A History of Wesleyan Methodism in Some of the Southern Counties of England* (1885)

Pepys, S., *Diary*

Gover, J.E.B., *The Place Names of Surrey* English Place Name Society Vol. XI C.U.P. (1934)

Postan, M.M., *The Medieval Economy and Society* Pelican (1975)

Pulford, J.S.L., *The First Kingston Quakers* (1973)

Rackham, O., *The History of the Countryside* Dent (1986)

Rowse, A.L., *Matthew Arnold – Poet and Prophet* Thames & Hudson (1976)

Stenton, D.M., *English Society in the Early Middle Ages* Pelican (1975)

Sheppard Frere, MA, FSA, *Report on the Roman Bath House at Chatley* Surrey Arch. Soc. Collections Vol. 50

Smith, R., *Romano-British Remains at Cobham* Surrey Arch. Soc. Collections Vols. 21 & 22

Stevenson, W., *Agriculture of Surrey* (1813)

Stider, D., *The Watermills of Surrey* Barracuda Books (1990)

Taylor, D.C., *Painshill Park* Esher News (1964 & 1971); *Methodism In Cobham* Esher News (1970); *When Cobham Nearly Had A Railway* Esher News (1970); *Looking Back at Cobham* Esher News (1972); *Cobham Park* Logica (1981); *Cobham Brewery – A Short History* (1981); *The Book of Cobham* Barracuda Books (1982); *The People of Cobham – The Pyports Connection* Barracuda Books (1985); *Cobham In Camera* Quotes (1986); *Old Mistral, Cobham: A 16th century Warrener's House identified* Surrey Arch. Soc. collections vol. 79 (1989); *Cobham Characters* Appleton Publications (1999); *Cobham Houses and Their Occupants* Appleton Publications (1999); *Gerrard Winstanley in Elmbridge* Appleton Publications (2000); *Downside – Another Look* Appleton Publications (2000); *"Well Furnished With Inns"* Appleton Publications (2002); *Cobham Park – A House by Roger Morris* Georgian Group Journal (forthcoming)

Thompson, F.M.L., *English Landed Society in the Nineteenth Century* Routledge and Keen (1963)

Trevor, M., *The Arnolds* The Bodley Head (1973)

Tye, W., *The Life Story of John Earley Cook* Esher News (1970); *The Fairmile Since The Nineties* Esher News (1969)

Victoria County History of Surrey

Vincent, E.R. (ed.), *Alfieri – Memoirs* Oxford (1961)

Walker, T.E.C., *Cobham: Manorial History* Surrey Arch. Soc. Collections Vol. 58; *The Chase of Hampton Court* Surrey Arch. Soc. Collections Vol. 62; *Cobham Incumbents and Curates* Surrey Arch. Soc. Collections Vol. 71; *The Diary of Admiral Graham Moore* Surrey Arch. Soc. Collections Vol. 60; *Cobham Spas* Esher District Local History Society Newsletter No. 34.

Ward, Mrs H., *A Writer's Recollections*

Warren, J. (ed.), *Wealden Buildings* Coach Publishing (1990)

Wesley, Rev. J., *Journals & Letters* Epworth Press (1909-16 Journals, and 1931 letters)

Whitworth, R., *Field Marshal Lord Ligonier* Oxford (1958)

Wright, T., *The Life of William Huntingdon S.S.* Farncombe & Son (1909)

Wilson, Geoffrey, *The Old Telegraphs* Phillimore (1976)

The Surrey Record Society has published a number of volumes with material that relates to Cobham. The volumes concerning the *Chertsey Cartulary*, the *Surrey Quarter Sessions*, the *Surrey Hearth Tax* and the *Surrey Eyre* have been consulted for this book as has *The Calendar of Assize Records – Surrey Indictments for the Reigns of Elizabeth I and James I* HMSO.

The chief sources for unpublished material relating to the history of Cobham can be found in the Surrey History Centre at Woking. Here are deposited many of the records relating both to the manor and parish as well as private land holdings and other documents. Other Cobham material can be found in the National Archives (formerly the Public Record Office) at Kew. Cobham library also has a small local history section.

Material from archaeological excavations undertaken in Cobham can be found in Elmbridge Museum at Weybridge and in Guildford Museum at Castle Arch which also houses the collections and library of the Surrey Archaeological Society.

Index

Page numbers printed in **bold** type refer to illustrations

Detail from John Rocque's map of Surrey showing Cobham and the surrounding area in the middle of the 18th century.